NADIA

SUSAN K. DOWNS &
SUSAN MAY WARREN

ISBN 1-59310-163-5

For more information about Susan K. Downs and Susan May Warren, please access the authors' Web sites at the following Internet addresses:
www.susankdowns.com
www.susanmaywarren.com

Acquisitions and Editorial Director: Rebecca Germany
Editorial Consultant: Becky Durost Fish
Art Director: Jason Rovenstine
Layout Design: Anita Cook

Published by Barbour Publishing, Inc., P.O. Box 719, Uhrichsville, Ohio 44683, www.barbourbooks.com

Our mission is to publish and distribute inspirational products offering exceptional value and biblical encouragement to the masses.

Printed in the United States of America
5 4 3 2 1

Susan K. Downs

Dedication:
In Christ there is no East or West, in him no South or North,
but one great fellowship of love throughout the whole wide earth.

—From the hymn,
"In Christ There Is No East or West,"
words by John Oxenham, 1908

Growing up as a child of the sixties in Oklahoma, I viewed the bomb/tornado drills as an integral part of my well-rounded education and preparation for life. To my first-grade mind, a Russian bomb was just as likely to fall from the sky as one of our trademark twisters. These drills came at regular intervals—every other month or so—but always at a time when we least expected them, intended to catch us with our guard down and our reactions slow.

Each time the continuous, ear-piercing trill of the school bell began, I wondered if this time the alert was for real and not a practice exercise. I remember wanting my mama oh-so-desperately when Mrs. Pierce instructed us to fall in line, in an orderly fashion, and move calmly yet swiftly into the hallway. Fear drove my heartbeat into a double-time pound as I squeezed between two classmates and huddled in the Myers Elementary hallway with my head between my knees. (As if that would protect us from a nuclear bomb!) Praying. Hoping. Waiting for the all-clear signal to sound.

I hated the Russians for scaring me. This was all those Soviet Communists' fault. Why did they want to hurt little American girls like me?

That latent fear, that dormant hatred, lingered for decades—until the inconceivable occurred and the Soviet Union crumbled along with its Communist government. We were missionaries in South Korea at the time, and soon after the Soviet Union morphed into the Commonwealth of Independent States, my husband made his first trip to Moscow to help establish a mission work there. He came home brimming with tales of wonderful encounters with the citizens of that once-enemy land. His depictions defied all I'd been taught to believe about America's Cold War nemesis. The people he described couldn't possibly hail from the same country I'd been conditioned to despise.

Then, I had the great fortune to experience Russia and her people for myself. In my work as an international adoption coordinator, I rode the trains into the snowy hinterlands, met with government officials, stayed in villagers' homes, worshiped with believers of likeminded faith—and made friends. To my amazement, I discovered we shared a lot more in common than we had in difference, these new friends and I.

I thank God for the privilege of living in the age of an ever-shrinking globe, for the gift of friends from other cultures and languages and lands. I dedicate that which is mine of *Nadia,* this Cold War-era story, to the generations of persecuted Christians who kept the faith—even when to do so meant risking their very lives. Great is their reward.

I looked and there before me was a great multitude that no one could count, from every nation, tribe, people, and language, standing before the throne and in front of the Lamb. They were wearing white robes and were holding palm branches in their hand. And they cried out in a loud voice: "Salvation belongs to our God, who sits on the throne, and to the Lamb."

—Revelation 7:9–10

Acknowledgments:

The thrill of seeing a new family born through the miracle of international adoption proved reward enough for those long hours of travel flying across the Atlantic. . .bouncing along unpaved roads. . .jerking over trans-Siberian rails. Still, I never would have guessed back then I'd see those exhausting Russian journeys as blessings in disguise.

Sincere thanks go to:

Lori Stahl, a special adoptive mother who, during her home-study interview, showed me a mysterious old graveside photo of her ancestors that started me thinking, *What if. . . ?*

Karen Jordan, Igor Korolev, Tatyana Terekhova, Marina Sokolova, and the rest of the team on the Russian side of our adoption work. Though we no longer work together, you'll always be like family to me.

My "spit-n-polish" partner, *Susan May Warren*, who shares my love of both Russian and heavenly things. I thank God for converging our paths.

Travis, Curtis, Kevin, Kimberly, and Courtney—whether through birth or adoption, when I became your mother, I knew I'd been blessed!

David, my beloved husband and partner in adventure, I can't wait to see where life's road takes us next.

SUSAN MAY WARREN

Dedication:
For Your glory, Lord!

Acknowledgments:

God has a sense of humor, and I experienced it firsthand as I wrote *Nadia,* the story of the spy racing through Russia, trying to bring her beloved home. I had spent the last year watching my husband struggle between his missionary calling and his family, just as Nadia did. Little did I know that once we determined God wanted us to move to America, our adventures were only beginning. I wrote *Nadia* while living in a 28 x 30-foot garage without running water or electricity (thank the Lord for laptop batteries). Easily, I conjured up the cold starkness of being in a gulag cell as winter descended outside our poorly insulated garage or sleeping in cramped places as we tucked our family of six into our popup camper. Most of all, I wondered at my purpose in life, now that I was no longer a missionary. I found joy in Mickey's understanding that only God could make his life significant and answers in Nadia's revelation that God would give her daily wisdom and work out His perfect will as she drew closer to Him. Most of all, God reminded me that I write each word by His grace. He will teach me and equip me to write for Him, even if it means putting me in a garage!

Among God's other provisions for this journey were the following people. I'm deeply grateful for their part in the making of *Nadia*:

Rebecca Germany, for believing in *Heirs of Anton* and for your enthusiasm and wisdom in crafting a story about a Russian family. We're so blessed by your support!

Susan Downs, my cowriter who knows how to take my words and polish them to a shine. Thank you for your wisdom and your encouragement.

Tracey, Chris, and Nancy, who kept me going with laughter and teasing, especially when the nights turned especially dark. You are bright lights in my life.

Valerie Gustafson, the Warren family tour guide. Thank you for embracing us and making us feel welcome. You were one of our first smiles.

Our new family at First Baptist Church in Grand Marais. Wow, to be counted as a part of your fellowship is a great and humbling honor. We rejoice to praise God beside you.

Pastor Dale and Linda McIntire. Your words of wisdom, from the pulpit or in conversation, prodded my heart and mind to understand the true meaning of wisdom. I thank the Lord for sending us to a place where we can be fed spiritually and emotionally. I told you all the good stuff you were sharing would end up in a book!

Andrew and the kiddos, my cheering section and fellow "sufferers." Thank you for your patience, for eating canned ravioli and boxed mac and cheese for five months, for listening to me ramble about CIA cold war intrigues, and, most of all, for enduring the "garage months" with grace and patience. You're a great bunch, and I'm so grateful for you!

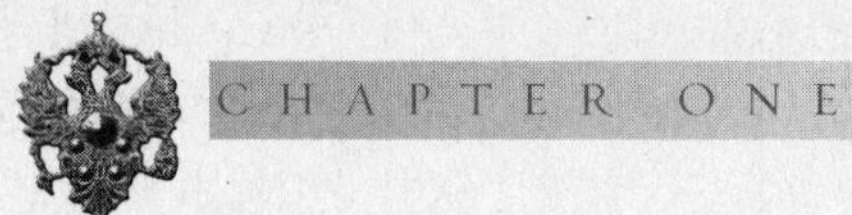

CHAPTER ONE

"For the LORD *is good and His love endures forever. His faithfulness continues through all generations."*
—PSALM 100

MOSCOW, 1970

Anyone looking at her might see a woman lost in the jazz, swaying to the sassy tones imported from America and emulated, often poorly, in a dingy underground nightclub on the south side of Moscow.

No one would recognize her as Hope, aka "Nadia," Moore, seasoned CIA agent, now poised on the edge of desperation. She gripped her stool with both hands and crossed one booted leg over the other, moving her foot to the music of Aretha Franklin sung by a long-haired Muscovite with an ear-aching accent.

Hope slung her gaze across the shadowed room, searching. No, he hadn't arrived. And no one had made her cover. Yet.

She sighed and leaned back against the bar. The low murmurs from clumped conversation groups tugged on her ears and competed against the racket onstage. These clandestine forums oozed information that might further the cause of the United States against their Cold War nemesis. Hope had been a habitual eavesdropper for too long.

Over the dark room, maybe twenty meters square,

hovered a cloud of smoke—cigarette and otherwise. Thankfully, Russia didn't have near the drug problem that ravaged the youth across the ocean. Still, possession of illegal substances netted a gruesome sentence in the gulags to the north—a prospect guaranteed to crash the highest high. Russia's drug of choice centered on the state-sanctioned firewater, vodka; and this close, its acrid redolence cramped Hope's empty stomach.

Oh, yeah. Food. She'd been too busy to eat. Too intent on sneaking into Russia. Too focused on saving the only man she'd ever loved.

She glanced at the timepiece that hung from a long chain around her neck. Aranoff was now over an hour late. Had he received her message? She'd left it in their former dead drop. Fear found a foothold and dug at her courage. She was an idiot to think he still checked his PO box or the chipped-out brick behind the Dumpster at his cousin's flat. She fingered the piece of jewelry, a wedding gift from Mickey. The backside contained a small compartment for microdots and other clandestine information she might courier.

Not today. This trip was about her. About Mickey.

About baby Ekaterina.

For the thirteen thousandth time in the last twenty hours, she called herself crazy, and her courage knotted into a hard ball in her stomach.

Crazy Hope. That's what she had.

Crazy Hope. That's what Mickey had called her when she'd snuck them into a General Assembly meeting of the Duma or when she'd secreted her way onto a Leningrad train and into the private berths of General Lashtoff. Her crazy, even fantastical missions—and accomplishments—had earned her legendary status in the company. But even she knew that springing Mickey out of Gorkilov Prison or even evading the KGB in this dimly lit underground cabaret might be a feat above Crazy Hope's abilities.

But she wasn't going to let Mickey die without demanding from him the truth.

Hope breathed out hard. Sweat beaded underneath her long, black wig. Twenty hours under its weight made her neck muscles scream. She should have waited to don her disguise until the Moscow airport. Then again, wouldn't it have seemed strange to see someone with ginger brown hair wearing the conservative shirtdress of a mother enter the bathroom, and a young, hip, dark brunette with waist-long hair and a beaded necklace exit? No, she needed the guise of American student and war protester to get her into the mass of society. Let customs officials see nothing more sinister than a free-love hippie with a peace agenda, and they'd let her pass without a blink. But a mother of one, a savvy woman with fluency in three languages and the ability to move around Russian society like a mouse? They'd have her under the bright light in the KGB bowels faster than Solzhenitsyn.

Once inside Russia, she'd beelined for the *Zhenshina Belaya Nocha,* her old stomping grounds, snuck in the back entrance, and changed into a more conservative, Russian-style dirt-brown polyester skirt, turquoise blouse, and suede jacket. Still hip. But tame enough to blend into the Soviet crowd.

Please, Aranoff, find me.

She turned around to the bartender, a gaunt man with an Adam's apple the size of Brooklyn, and ordered a tomato juice. He eyed her, perhaps a moment too long, and slid her the drink.

She drank it down in one gulp and felt it saturate her

insides with nourishment. Once, on a mission to plant a bug in the inner office of a high-ranking party secretary, she'd gone without eating for over two days.

She would gladly never eat again if it meant Mickey might live.

A new song by a new jazz singer. This time the music of John Coltrane filled the room. The shaggy heads of Moscow University students, who pushed the party line with their neck-length hair and fringed leather jackets, stared at the musician. No movement. No swaying of heads. No feet tapping in time to the music.

Even in their attempts to reproduce the West, they couldn't break free of stoic Soviet culture. Hope stopped her bobbing foot. Her heart sank. How quickly she'd forgotten her training, relaxed her instincts. If the KGB hadn't spotted her yet and weren't rounding up a posse outside the *Belaya*'s doors, it would only be due to God's mercy.

She hoped God was especially generous with said mercy on this trip. Then again, she hadn't really spent any time considering Him until Ekaterina was born. Until a year ago, God had been stories told by her grandmother, an ethereal, maybe protective thought in the back of her brain. Having a baby had put the need for God into her life, had occasionally sent her eyes heavenward. All the same, He felt as far away as upstate New York, distant from her problems, her life of espionage.

Maybe she hadn't earned the right to mercy. . . .

And Mickey's credentials were shaky at best.

The truth was, why would God care about a couple of desperate spies who certainly hadn't earned a place of honor in His holy roll call?

No, maybe they were all on their own. And if so, she

was certainly in over her head.

Aranoff, where are you?

She stood, walked over to the wall, leaned one shoulder into it, and surreptitiously scanned the room. A blond, tucked in the shadows stage left, caught her attention. Hope's heart skipped when she noted the woman had her in her sights. No smile, her eyes fixed. Recognition slid over Hope like a chill.

Lena.

Mickey's friend.

Or should she say. . .*girlfriend?*

Hope fought the anger that welled at the back of her throat. Lena should be wasting away on death row in Mickey's place. And if Hope could figure out a way to make the *swallow*—the KGB femme fatale—pay for her crimes, she'd invest a lifetime into bringing her to justice.

Focus. Hope blew out a breath. She was here for Ekaterina. And she wouldn't jeopardize her mission—even for revenge.

Where is Aranoff?

The fear that he'd been arrested flickered across her brain, and she winced. No. She would have heard. Aranoff Chornov was too valuable to disappear without a ripple in the community. Even her father, as angry as he still was over her marriage, would have eased his stance and conveyed the news that one of her best friends had been betrayed.

No, only Mickey was doing the betraying these days. A fact that her father, spymaster Edward Neumann, took every opportunity to drive home.

She held up her glass, hoping for one last taste of juice, and noticed her hand shook. Her own softness rattled her. Two years out of the field, and she reacted like a rookie.

Maybe she was. Maybe she'd been out of the game so long that this attempt to salvage her future was sheer suicide. Then where would Ekaterina be?

An orphan.

Hope closed her eyes and let the image of her one-year-old—the baby-soft caramel-colored hair, the amber brown eyes, the droolly smile—wax her mind. A softness started in her heart and spread out through her body. No. She wouldn't fail. She'd bring home Kat's father. And then, somehow, she'd start being the mother she should be.

Whatever that meant.

Somehow, she had to believe that yanking Mickey out of this mess held the key to her questions, to this sudden floundering for identity. Ever since she'd held her red-faced squirming daughter in her arms, an unfamiliar feeling had sizzled in her chest.

She'd finally named it. *Panic.*

She, the woman who knew how to sweet-talk the German Stasi into allowing her into a covert restaurant for party officials, the same operator who could unlock a closed door in less than ten seconds, felt just a little weak every time her daughter toddled up to her, arms out, toothless mouth grinning.

She needed this trip if only to find her footing. Resurrect the confidence that had shattered into smithereens on the floor of a Nyack, New York, maternity ward.

She put the glass down and crossed her arms over her chest, pushing her fear into a cold ball. She refused to believe the rumors until she could confront her lying, traitorous, two-timing husband face-to-face.

So maybe she believed the rumors more than she wanted to admit.

Two minutes out in the back alley with the woman across the room, and Hope would have the hard, cold facts.

Somehow, that only sent a ripple of pure fear up her spine.

No, she'd wait until she could look square into Mickey's light green eyes, see past the legends, the cover stories, and reveal the truth.

And maybe, if she really kept her wits about her, she'd be able to withstand his intoxicating charisma long enough to convince him to return home. To her.

To Kat.

Don't expect loyalty from a career spy, Nadezhda. Her father's voice took out a chunk of her heart with one swoop, and she gasped. No. She'd pledged to trust Mickey.

And she would.

Even if his girlfriend sat across the room like a minx, oozing elegance and charm and 120 percent deceit.

Oh Mickey, how could you?

As if in some mystical trance, Hope couldn't rip her gaze off the woman, her long, nearly white-blond hair, the way she laughed with others at her table. Hope felt a hot ball ignite in her chest when the woman looped an arm through one of her companions and whispered into his ear. Lena still had the poise of a ballerina, the figure of Marilyn Monroe.

Lena Chornova obviously hadn't given birth to a nine-pound baby within the last year. Hope felt downright pudgy in her dingy skirt. Little wonder Mickey had moved on.

No. He'd pledged to love her, too.

Hadn't he?

She pushed off the wall when Lena exited during the rhythmic applause following a Duke Ellington tune. Hope eased over to the opposite door, and her heart in her throat, she debated tailing the little tramp. Aranoff hadn't shown, and Lena was a sure link to the only man who could help Hope. Besides, suddenly Hope couldn't bear another moment of not knowing.

"Nadia Neumann. Welcome back to the USSR."

Hope turned, and her heart jumped into her throat. Dressed in head-to-toe black garb and smoking a cigarette stood the very picture of her nightmares.

Komitet Gosudarstvennoy Bezopasnosti. . .the KGB.

The KGB didn't hold a prayer of breaking him. Not after 382 days and six hours of imprisonment. Not with their beatings. Not with the threats of reprisal against his wife or his fellow agents. Not even with the loneliness that came from shivering, night after long night, in a dank, two-by-two-meter cell.

No, the Siberian cold would kill him first.

Michael, aka "Misha," aka "Mickey," aka "World-Class Failure" Moore huddled in a ball and watched the snow angle through the shoe-box–sized hole fifteen feet above his head and drift lazily, as if mocking him, to the floor, where it had begun to accumulate. He pushed his bare toe into the fluffy mound and closed his eyes against a wave of dread when he felt nothing. Stripped to only his thin, holey prison pants, he'd discovered that this new torture technique had its positives—namely a hypothermic, painless death. The end to a year of pain. Of empty hopes. Of wondering if he might live until tomorrow.

Tomorrows that, according to inside sources, were going to end in three days.

If the frigid winter night didn't kill him first.

He'd long since stopped dreaming he might live to be reunited with Hope.

Michael leaned his grimy head against the cement wall, feeling his teeth rattle against the cold. He didn't deserve to see her again, even if he somehow managed to escape, a possibility that felt farther from his grip every day.

At least he would die without having revealed his ring of agents and operatives who worked in the Soviet Union, hoping to keep the Cold War from boiling over. Contacts that included his wife. He might be a lousy husband, a rotten handler, and an even worse operator, but every cell and fiber in his skin-and-bones body was a to-the-death patriot. If he could do but one thing right, he would die well. With his country's secrets trapped in his brain.

He heard the rattle of a metal cup against cement. Evgeny, awake. Michael and his neighbor had bridged the communication barrier with Morse code, which told Michael that Evgeny had been a soldier of some sort. He had a wife, a grown daughter, and had worked as an engineer in Moscow. Beyond that, Michael knew that Evgeny was a fighter. More than once, Michael had seen the guy dragged back to his cell looking more like reindeer sausage than a human being. Still, Evgeny rose from the grip of death to tap on the floor and give Michael hope.

Hope that came in the form of Bible verses.

Sixty days into his incarceration, Michael had unraveled the laborious sentence his neighbor tapped out in the wee hours of the night. "Be strong and courageous. For the Lord your God is with you."

Right then, hope lit an ember in his heart. One that

refused to die, despite the KGB's brutal attempts to snuff it out.

Maybe, just maybe, God hadn't abandoned the spy with a hundred names. The man who wove a web of deceit so thick, he couldn't remember the way back to the truth. He'd begun his spy days with a noble purpose, even found fuel for it in the proverbs embedded in his brain. *"Rescue those being led away to death; hold back those staggering toward slaughter."* His Bible drills as a child in Ohio told him that standing up for right against evil counted in the kingdom of heaven. But ten years fighting an unseen war left him raw, weary, and wondering if he'd etched out even a toehold for righteousness.

He could point out way too many moments when righteousness had been the last thing on his mind. And 382 days of painful labor and no rescue attempt told just what kind of legacy he'd created.

However, since meeting Evgeny, he'd begun to hope that God offered redemption and a final purpose for the man who once had it all. . .and had chucked it without looking back. Until, of course, he realized what he had lost.

How Michael longed to replay time and return to that moment when he had a choice. This time, he would take the road that led him into Hope's arms. Regret seemed a living being, crawling through his chest on the dark nights when she visited him in his dreams.

Still, perhaps if he stayed the course, God could redeem his calling, give light to his dismal life. In his death, he'd be the man he should have been in life. A man who protected the woman he loved.

Three days to his execution.

Maybe someday Hope would find the one thing he'd given her that could prove that her husband had been a patriot who had loved her to the grave.

"Cold," Evgeny tapped.

Michael pried his hand off his bare knee, and amazed at the cold that rushed in its wake, he found his own cup. "*Da,*" he returned.

"News from home." Evgeny's tapping reverberated through the hall, but no guards ventured into the frozen, cement wasteland to torment the rebels. "Larissa married."

Michael winced, and the texture of his own fatigue and loss rubbed tears into his eyes. Poor man. Missed his own daughter's wedding. Thankfully, Michael didn't have a daughter to steal his heart and dash it against his regrets.

"Congratulations," he tapped, feeling the emptiness of his word.

"Thank you," Evgeny answered, ever the polite Russian, even in his own private agony. "Wife. Visit. Soon."

Yeah, right. The possibility of Evgeny's wife visiting him, even *finding* him in the middle of Russia seemed as farfetched as Michael enjoying a good dinner this Thanksgiving. "Great," he tapped, playing along with the lie.

"Don't give up."

The sound reverberated across the pane of night, against the cold, and into Michael's soul. He sighed and this time felt hot tears parting his frozen cheeks. The snowfall, backdropped by the glaring yard lights, reflected an eerie orange glow into the room, as if lighting it afire, and Michael had the strangest sense of warmth. If only he could really, truly hang onto hope. But he felt so dangerously near surrendering to the urge to curl into a ball and let the cold arrange his escape.

No more beatings. No more regrets. No more temptation to agree to their promises of release in exchange for names.

No more memories tearing his heart in half of Hope coming to him. There were times, moments between the pain, the cold, and the hunger, when he closed his eyes, and her image blanketed his mind, soothing, salving the anguish with tender memories. Those golden brown eyes, dancing with mischief and laughter. That long, ginger brown hair, sun streaked and falling between his fingers like silk. Her hand in his, *Mickey. . .trust me. . . . I love you. . . .*

His gut churned. Look where it had gotten her. A widow at age twenty-nine.

At least she was young enough to marry again.

What was he thinking? She'd probably headed back to America, annulled their marriage, and had already found happiness in the arms of another man. Not that she was fickle in her love—but rather, wise. She probably came to her senses and realized ten minutes after he left town that "Mickey" meant "Mistakey." But the thought of another man inhaling her fragrance, on the receiving end of her laughter. . .fire shot through him, the first glimpse that he might live through this night. He raised his eyes to heaven, tears freezing on his cheeks. "I wronged her, Lord. I know it. Please, give her a man whom she can trust, who is faithful, and who can love her the way she deserves. Give her a man who will protect and honor her and keep his promises."

His throat grew raw. Yes, someone who might protect her. From herself.

Deep inside, he half-expected Crazy Hope to storm the prison and attempt his escape.

That scared him more than anything the KGB could dish out.

Because if they caught her. . .well, all he'd spent the last decade hiding would come out in a rush.

The one sure way to make him confess in spades—his Hope in the clutches of the KGB.

CHAPTER TWO

"Nadia Moore. I'm married, remember?" Nadia stuffed her heart back into her chest and formed a mock glare intended to disguise the fact that Aranoff had scared her out of her skin. She still fought her racing heartbeat. "And you're late."

"Not late. Just scoping out the place. You'll find your local KGB leaning against the wall, smoking Cubans by the door." Aranoff nodded toward them while moving beside her as if ignoring her. "And yes, I remember you're married."

She spared him a glance, and again, his tight jaw, etched cheekbones, nearly pale blue eyes, and dark-as-mink hair sent a shock through her. If Mickey hadn't stolen her heart, this Russian, one of her best friends for nearly a decade, would have easily caught it up and wound it around his strong fingers. What was it about KGB Colonel Aranoff Chornov that made her feel safe. . .yet slightly afraid?

He scanned the room. "I have a car in the alley."

She inched toward the door and, a few moments later, slipped into the back hall. Retrieving her backpack from a niche behind the coal furnace, she strode to the exit and left the building. The smell of fall spiced the air, along with the sweet crispness of an impending storm. Blue lights bathed the street, but in the alley, only the intermittent moonlight illuminated the shapes. She found the sedan—a KGB Black Maria—and slid into the backseat, crouching low in the well between seats. The acrid taste of fear lined her mouth. The perfect refuge—inside the enemy's lair. The realization ran gooseflesh down her arms. The cold nipped at her knees, found her hands, and she shoved them into her pockets, fighting a shiver. For a fleeting moment, she wondered where this night might find Mickey. Was he warm, snuggled under a woolen blanket? Her throat tightened as Aranoff strode out of the building, glanced down the alley, then crossed to the car.

He said nothing as he entered. A slightly sweet smell of smoke tracked him in, along with the traces of his aftershave and wool coat. He didn't look her way but started the Maria and rolled down the alley and out into the street.

Nadia crouched under the windows, staring out at the gray cement buildings leering above her, screaming discovery. She saw faces silhouetted in the windows, nameless Russians smoking cigarettes or staring into the night wearing blank expressions, as if overwhelmed by tomorrow. In times like these, she understood the Russian soul. The helplessness of living in a society bulwarked by the double pillars of deceit and bribery. Instead of safeguards, Soviet rules loomed like a guillotine waiting to decimate the public. The average Russian hadn't a hope of dodging trouble, only bribing their way out of it—scraping up enough rubles *naleva* to avoid gulag. No wonder alcoholism started in the middle grades and cut the average life span to fifty. She had forgotten how the despair of the collective Russian soul had infiltrated her heart.

She'd felt like a prisoner freed from her shackles when she'd left.

Or perhaps it had been the duplicity of her own devising that had kept her imprisoned.

She shivered again, wondering if she possessed the raw grit, the savvy, and pure luck needed to spring Mickey.

Aranoff turned off *Kalinina* Prospect and wound down *Ylitsa Zapparena.* Nadia recognized the stately Stalin-era buildings. Burnt orange and yellow in daylight, with ornate moldings and seven-foot-tall windows, now they resembled the eyes of the Soviet: one mind watching the spy huddled in the backseat. She closed her eyes.

Nope, bad idea. Fatigue rushed over her. She forced herself awake in time to feel the car stop. "Get out," Aranoff said without turning.

She knew the drill. Opening the door, she jumped out, slammed it, then started a brisk walk in the opposite direction. *Down to the corner, turn left, half a block, cut through the alleyway, double back down another side street, around a bank of metal garages, through a tiny park, and then up the back stairs of an old, wooden apartment building.*

As she entered the two-story, Lenin-era building, cobwebs hung from the walls, cement flaked off the lath and plaster, and the odor of dog urine invaded her nose like a sentry, as if trying to block her advance into this pocket of common society. She held her breath and nearly ran up the two flights of stairs, careful to skip the third step from the top lest the whine awaken everyone in the building.

Her skeleton key still worked, and she wrestled with the door only a second before she slipped into the cold, dank, two-room flat.

She knew her way through the darkness and easily found the window, pulling the heavy drapes closed. Then, dropping her backpack onto the table, she found the lamp and turned on the light.

A cascade of luminescence poured over the brown-painted wooden floor, the red-and-black patterned divan, the straight-backed chairs, and table. The place still smelled moldy, as if someone had forgotten to air it out since the Bolshevik Revolution, and she saw at least three dead roaches curled on their backs in the corner.

Home sweet home.

No, her home had been on the north side, a one-room efficiency filled with Mickey's laughter, his smile, his ready-for-adventure aura. She'd held down the rent for two months after he left. . .and then packed up their life and headed back to New York.

Believing, wrongly in retrospect, that Mickey would follow her.

She never once dreamed she'd have to leave their daughter in the care of her grandma and fly to Russia to spring her husband from a Russian jail. Never.

Or that she'd find herself back inside Aranoff's safe house. She rubbed her arms and fought a wave of despair. For the first time since returning to Russia, she longed for the quiet, boring evenings spent bouncing her daughter on her lap.

She nearly jumped out of her wig when the door cracked open. Aranoff entered without looking at her, shut the door, and locked it. She held her breath a moment, the silence dredging up memories. She remembered the first time she hid here. Nearly eight years ago during the KGB raids on suspected sleepers in Moscow connected with double-agent Oleg Rustikoff. As they'd burned a singular candle and ate cold herring and brown bread, Mickey kept Nadia's spirits buoyed with stories and jokes, diverting her imagination from friends and colleagues arrested and tortured in the dungeons of Lubyanka.

Even then, she supposed, she loved him. Michael Moore, legendary handler, adventurer, Mr. Sassy Appeal-Mystery-and-Charm rolled into a boy-next-door package of rangy muscles, lazy green eyes, and unruly reddish brown hair. Yum. Unfortunately, Mickey regarded her as a zealous *redskin,* a tourist with a taste for espionage. He didn't view her as a professional equal until years after she became a courier, then a cutout, going between his various operators with clandestine messages.

She easily recalled the day he began to take her seriously.

She closed her eyes, letting herself relax in the feeling of his arms around her, the smell of his leather coat, and harsh rub of the whiskers shadowing his face.

"Nadia." Aranoff strode across the room, and she opened her eyes a second before he swept her into his arms. "I'm so glad you're safe."

Her legs went weak as she reeled herself out of the memory of Mickey and into the embrace of Aranoff. He felt rugged and strong, and she wrapped her arms around his waist and held on tight. How could she have ever doubted his loyalty? Shame boiled in her gut that she'd even entertained, however briefly on the airplane, the thought that Aranoff had betrayed his handler to the KGB. After all, wasn't he Mickey's best friend long before he'd turned double-agent?

"Thank you for meeting me, Aranoff," she said, gathering her courage. "I know you took a risk."

The lamplight illuminated his pale blue eyes, always searching, always heavy with the texture of concern. Her heart softened, wondering what would have happened had she not been Mickey's girl.

"I'd do anything for you."

She sat on the sofa next to him and eked out a smile as she worked her wig off her head. The rush of cool air against her sweaty temples swept the cotton from her brain, and she shook out her bobbed hair, running her fingers through it, massaging away the final layer of exhaustion. She needed sleep, but devising a master plan meant she needed to keep her eyes open, her mind sharp.

Aranoff watched her as she leaned forward, propped her elbows on her knees, folded her hands, and looked him in his kind eyes. "How do you feel about helping me spring Mickey out of the clink?"

He smiled, and it looked like pure danger. "I thought you'd never ask."

Relief rushed through her in a hot gust. "Thank you, Aranoff. I know you're risking your life."

"Mickey's worth it." Behind his eyes, Nadia saw him scrolling through the many times Mickey had diverted KGB suspicions, saving Aranoff's cover, not to mention his life. "I'd do just about anything for him, too."

"I know." Nadia touched his hand. "Do you know. . . how he was caught?"

He swallowed, looked away, and anguish creased his face. It told her he suffered knowing his best friend had been swallowed into the KGB archipelago. "Someone betrayed him. He returned safely from Kazakhstan, and just after he made his drop, they picked him up."

"Do you know what mission he was on?"

His expression turned grim. "RORSAT."

Shock took a swipe at her stomach, and she swallowed hard. "Arsenal's project?"

Aranoff nodded. "Tested it last year. They launched it last January."

"Is it nuclear?" She held her breath. She knew the Russians had a radar ocean reconnaissance satellite in the works. Designed to track the United States Navy from space, the system already struck fear in the hearts of analysts sitting in the basement of the Pentagon. But if it went nuclear—well, the world might as well prepare for nuclear winter. The thought of one hundred pounds of enriched uranium falling from the sky to scatter radioactive particles across whatever country fate might choose froze the blood of leaders on both sides of the ocean. Obviously, the Russians didn't give the slightest nod toward a little agreement entitled the 1963 Nuclear Test Ban Treaty.

"The US-A wasn't nuclear. It used chemical batteries, according to Mickey's report. But they have another in the works. He said he got shots of it. The Cosmos 469. Equipped with a BES-5 nuclear reactor."

She sat back on the sofa as chills raised gooseflesh. "Okay. So he got caught with some Russian space secrets. Why then is HQ calling him a defector?"

She'd tried to muscle this information out of her father, but Edward Neumann hadn't been a lifetime spy for his predilection toward betraying secrets. It felt a bit like trying to pry open Fort Knox.

"Misha betrayed the sleepers."

She stared at him as every nerve in her body went cold. "The entire ring?"

"No. Just Wilson and Sukharov."

Nadia closed her eyes. She remembered Tommy Wilson well. A round-faced journalist with the *Baltimore Times*. He'd given her and Mickey a jar of black caviar for their wedding. She felt Aranoff's hand on hers, but she couldn't move. How could Mickey have betrayed the agents he risked his life for over the past ten years? He was their handler, their connection with the agency, their lifeline in the country. To betray them was to become Judas to Jesus. No. She'd seen him, too many times, risk his life for those secrets. He'd die before he unlocked them for the KGB.

Unless, of course, they had devised a torture technique even Mickey couldn't fight.

She felt sick, opened her eyes, and squeezed Aranoff's hand. "He didn't betray his agents, Aranoff. I don't believe it."

Aranoff covered their clasped hands and leaned forward, eyes studying hers. "I don't believe it, either."

She nodded, feeling wrung out. "We gotta get him out."

Aranoff pinched his lips and wore a look that made her insides tight. Instinctively, she braced herself.

"They ordered his execution date."

No. Her fears rose with a haunting moan. *No!* It could not end this way. "I can't sit by and watch him die, Aranoff."

"Of course not." He let go of her hand, rubbed the back of his fingers against her cheek. "Just leave everything to me."

He recognized it as a dream. Even so, he settled into it, relishing the sounds, the warmth, the sweetness it churned up in his chest. He hungered for these REM moments, so few they'd become, and when they happened, he knew it was a gift.

This time, the images felt familiar, as if dredged up

from the back of his brain and tossed together with his dreams into the magic of subconsciousness. Yes, it had to be a memory, because they were on the train. He heard the familiar rattle as the car jolted with the rhythm of the wheels and smelled the musty seats, the sour odor of vodka and fish that his compartment mates spread out on the tiny table between bunks. Aranoff was there, across from him, his wide-whiskered smile cultivating trust, his pale blue eyes as sharp as a wolf's. He lifted his vodka glass, toasted to the soldier in the opposite berth. In his dream, Mickey knew what would happen next, even braced himself as the compartment door clicked, then opened. Still, when she stopped by his door, he felt something give inside.

What was Nadia doing on a train bound for Leningrad? And dressed in the guise of a tea and treats vendor? She wore the standard green uniform of the Soviet railroad—never mind that on her, it actually looked fabulous—and she'd piled her ginger brown hair into a ball on her head. She wore little makeup but enough to accentuate her delicious, even sassy brown eyes. He felt a little sick when she smiled at the group, not letting recognition flicker in her eyes, and offered them tea and cookies.

He'd give her tea and cookies. Right before he shipped her back to the States. Edward Neumann's voice rang in his ears. "Don't let anything happen to her, Michael. She's your responsibility."

Great. Just great. Exactly what he wanted, a feisty spy who was going to get him fired, if not pulverized, when Neumann found out his only daughter had turned full-fledged operator. Mickey had specifically ordered her to stay at Moscow University, under her redskin cover. But here she was, looking and sounding the part of Russian servant, and it took all his training not to strangle her on the spot.

She served them sweetly, and without so much as a glance his way, she left. He groaned, or maybe it was simply in his sleep, but his eyes lingered in the space where she'd been.

She was dogging Colonel Lashtoff. He knew it. The man had been trailing Oleg Rustikoff for nearly six months, and with the net closing, she intended to unearth just what and how much the KGB had on America's very generous Russian defector.

If she didn't get killed first. Aranoff clamped him hard on the shoulder, his voice slightly slurred. "Misha, she's not your type. Too scholarly."

In the recesses of his brain, he recognized Aranoff's subtle warning to let her go. But fury or perhaps curiosity had him excusing himself and following her down the hall.

He caught up to her between two cars where the rubber walls gave slack insulation. Muscling her cart between the two doors kept her from hearing him as he snuck up behind her. He grabbed her about the waist and pulled her back into the car and into the bathroom.

"What?" She'd turned with the vehemence of a lynx and nearly decked him.

"Hey!" He dodged her and grabbed her arm. "What did you expect? That I'd let you saunter into Lashtoff's compartment without a nod?"

"Hi, Mickey." She smiled, her eyes twinkling, and he groaned. Why, oh why, did she call him Mickey? Like the cartoon mouse. He felt about thirteen every time she said it, especially in front of other agents. Like he might be a pet instead of a seasoned agent they depended on for their lives.

"Misha—and don't 'Hi' me. What are you doing here?"

She twisted her arm out of his grip, her smile still held in place. "Helping."

"Yeah, helping me right into my early grave." He surveyed her outfit. Yeah, she would have no problem wheedling her way into Lashtoff's private berth. He'd never seen a Russian tea lady so. . .

Okay, no, he shouldn't be entertaining thoughts about how good Hope Neumann looked in anything, nor the way the glint in her eyes made him wonder what devious plot simmered within that working brain of hers. She always scared him just a little, and now was definitely one of those times when he had to ignore the way she turned him to Jell-O and had to behave like her boss.

"I want you to go home," he said.

Her smile faded, and she looked uncannily like *his* boss, Edward Neumann, especially when he was given bad news. Which he never took well. "Yeah, sure. After I see the Hermitage."

"Next stop."

"No. We need this information. Rustikoff needs to leave if they're closing the noose."

"There are other ways." The bathroom felt about two inches wide and shrinking, with her braced against the door and him backed into the corner next to the window. She had her arms crossed over her chest and just enough of a pout to look every bit the twenty-year-old college student with a mischievous streak. For a second, he wanted more than anything to forget that she was under his care, take her in his arms, and—

"Yeah, slower and less effective ways," she retorted, totally unaware of his thundering heartbeat, the sweat building on his temples. "Let me sneak in there and see what I can dredge up."

He braced his arm against the wall over her shoulder as the train lurched. Her smell, something fresh and far too enticing, went straight to his brain. This bathroom was way, way too small. "I don't want you dredging up anything."

She looked past him, out the window, where the summer was turning back to spring as they headed north. "You're just playing watchdog for my father."

He cringed. "Yeah, well, your dad could do serious damage to my career, let alone my body, if anything happened to you." His gaze purposely tracked down her body, then met her eyes. They had widened at his bold perusal. "And I mean anything. Lashtoff has a reputation, and I don't want you anywhere near him."

She swallowed, and he could nearly see her scraping up the famous Neumann stubbornness. *Oh, no.*

"Well, thank you, my hero, but nothing is going to happen to me. And you can tell my dad to get used to it. I'm tired of sitting on the sidelines. I'm going to follow in the Neumann family footsteps."

He leaned away from her. "You do this, and I'll send you home so fast you'll get windburn on the plane."

"Hardly." She tapped him on the chest with her long, elegant hand. "You need me." And then she waggled her eyebrows and gave him a smile he still regretted. "Just trust me, will ya?"

She turned and yanked the door open.

He'd stood there like a dummy, still reeling from the way she'd put her hand on his chest, wondering if she'd felt his heart ricocheting off his ribs.

Then she disappeared. Dread filled his gut. He'd wandered back to his compartment, watched Aranoff exchange vodka shots and information with the naval commander with whom they'd managed to finagle a compartment, and sat in sick silence, just waiting for the KGB to run down the aisle in their hurry to execute Hope Neumann.

The next morning as they chugged into the Leningrad terminal, he descended to the platform and held his breath. No KGB waiting in a death huddle for their prey, only the obligatory soldiers standing with AK-47s, surveying the passengers. A cloud of coal smoke hung in the air, pigeons fought for sunflower shells, and passengers trudged toward the exits. He stood against the wall, letting Aranoff mingle with their targets. His chest felt like a knotted ball of nerves. When Nadia stepped out of a car at the end of the platform, her long hair in a ponytail, wearing a brown cashmere sweater and an A-line skirt, looking head-to-toe like a young American tourist, he wanted to sing. She sashayed past him, winked, and he nearly fainted.

Overhead, the sun parted the clouds and warmed him clear through to his heart.

It was this heat that woke him. He startled to see a guard standing over him, a flashlight in his face. He couldn't make out the expression, but somehow he knew that a prison guard waking him in the wee hours of the night couldn't mean anything good. What was worse, this looked like a new guy. Fresh. Not yet tired of beating him.

Oh, joy.

The man dragged him up, threw him against the wall. Mickey lay there, his nerves exploding, and stared up at his persecutor. "What?"

"She's back."

Mickey frowned and braced himself for the kick that came. He doubled over and wasn't sure whether to protect his head or his stomach.

But the blow took away his breath, a million times worse than physical punishment. The guard squatted next to him, his voice a low hiss.

"Nadezhda. And it's only a matter of time before we bring her in."

He stood then and laughed. And Mickey knew he would never be warm again.

CHAPTER THREE

Nadia had forgotten the nip of the Siberian cold, the one that came just before winter chomped down hard, a time when a few hardy leaves still clung to birch trees, when snow dusted the night, only to be erased by the day. Nadia huddled in the cold Zhiguli. The vinyl seats offered no warmth as night enshrouded her, seeping frost through the cracks of the squatty sedan.

Where Aranoff had scrounged up the transportation still seemed fuzzy. As did the last twenty-four hours. She vaguely remembered sleeping in the second-class *plascard* compartment of the train to Leningrad, too exhausted to let the prying eyes of her fellow sojourners rob her from the precious moments of unadulterated slumber. She let Aranoff, seated three seats down and facing her, watch her backpack while she escaped into unconsciousness.

She fought to claw out of the repose when the train lurched to a halt just south of Leningrad, in the city of Gorlosk. She gathered up her backpack and stumbled out, her eyes adjusting to the twilight that waxed the stately lime green train depot in shadow. Aranoff disembarked one car down and strode around the train station without a glance in her direction. Nadia gulped a calming breath, stood on the cement platform, and stared at the statue of Lenin—his arm extended, his bronze finger pointed west, as if directing her back onto the train and out of his country.

That felt about right. Her heart had already decided to head for home. Sometime after Aranoff left her at his safe house, the foolishness of her mission grabbed her about the throat and nearly choked off her air supply. What was she doing? Even Aranoff had voiced his doubts that they'd be able to break into Gorkilov Prison and free Russia's prize CIA spymaster.

She was a dead woman, and her daughter was an orphan.

What was worse, Mickey would be furious when he found out she'd risked her neck yet again.

She'd hiked her backpack over her shoulder, forced her eyelids open, blinking away the sleep, and wandered out to the street. Autumn breezes had stripped the birch trees down to bleached spires. The saggy-roofed, two-story, forest green apartment buildings, windows covered with steamy plastic, and the tinge of burning coal on the air evidenced the coming winter. She thought of the farmhouse in Schenectady, New York. The maples would be a brilliant red, the oaks a gilded bronze. The anticipation of sledding and ice-skating and Christmas felt strangely absent from this village. No pumpkins on the stoops, no scarecrows hanging limply in the kitchen gardens, not even the smell of leaves burning. Only the cold grip of dread. Winter wasn't a season taken lightly in Russia.

She remembered well the breath-stealing cold of a northern gust burning her lungs and pinching her nose as she trudged down Lenin Prospect, huddled in her faux mink *shuba* on the way to class at Moscow University. And the sound of Mickey's laughter as he chased her through Gregarin Park as the sun turned the snow and ice to diamonds. Yes, once Michael Moore surrendered to his emotions, the man had turned winter into a romantic, even sizzling playground.

Nadia shivered and shoved her hands into her pockets, forming fists as she turned and stalked down the street, purposely nowhere.

Aranoff picked her up six blocks later in a white, nondescript Zhiguli sedan.

They'd driven in silence out of town to the prison, a gray-bricked, four-story building surrounded by rutted earth and weed patches that had the smell and demeanor of suffering. A barbed-wire fence ran out from one end of the building, down one side, and around the back. A broken cement path led up to the building and around to the street, where a semipaved parking lot fought the weeds for possession. They drove by the building twice before Aranoff found a spot just on the other side of the forest that insulated the town from the gulag.

She rubbed a tiny hole in the window where her breath had obscured her view of Aranoff. He stood thirty feet away, ensconced in shadow, meeting with his contact in the niche of a poplar tree. Her heartbeat thundered in the background, and she gulped in a breath, fingering the wad of hundreds she'd smuggled into the country for precisely this purpose. She wasn't stupid. And she wasn't rich. But she knew she'd need a tidy bankroll to subvert Russian pride. If she could just entice one of the guards. . .

Aranoff strode back to the car in giant strides. He looked grim, dressed in head-to-toe black, his collar turned up against his hard jaw, his eyes down. He clasped his gloved hands together as if holding onto slim hope. She braced herself for the worst. Aranoff had put his life on the line, exposing his infidelity before the KGB with a brazenness that betrayed just how much Mickey meant to him. She looked skyward, to where the clouds obscured the stars, and prayed that God had sent them a disgruntled guard.

Aranoff got in the car and closed the door so the dome light would flicker out. "He'll do it."

Nadia's heart nearly leapt from her chest. "He'll let us sneak in?"

"Even better. He'll lead Mickey out." He looked straight ahead, not turning toward her.

Nadia stared at him, shock burying her words.

"He wants the entire five thousand, however."

She dug into her pocket, her hand curling around her life savings. "Should I give it to him?"

Aranoff shook his head and held out his hand. She passed him the wad of cash, and he shoved it into his coat pocket. "Better if you stay low. I'll pass it off. . .and then I'm leaving. I don't want Mickey to know I was here."

He looked at her then, those blue eyes full of worry. "He'll only be angry that I was involved."

What he left unspoken was at whom Mickey would be angry. Namely, her. She'd jeopardized one of America's most useful moles. Aranoff's information had helped them whisk endangered spies out of the country, had armed them in the face of Cold War deceptions, and overall kept the balance of powers on an even keel. Aranoff would be executed without a pause if the hounds in Lubyanka sniffed out his deception.

"Okay. I understand," Nadia said. "What next?"

"I'll deliver the cash, you drive me back into town, and I'll take the train back to Moscow." He touched her arm with his gloved hand, swallowed. "In the glove box, you'll find a train ticket and Russian passport for Mickey. I'll leave visa papers in your PO box in Moscow. You get there, pick them up, and I'll have someone meet you at the crossing to Finland."

Nadia mentally traced the route. Twice she'd helped agents out through the safe house on the Finnish border. She nodded.

"You look cold." He took off his glove, touched her cheek. Longing rose in his eyes, and it sent a wave of unease through her. She knew how he felt about her. He had made it clear shortly after Mickey left for Kazakhstan, despite the fact she had recently married. He still hadn't accepted her answer, given over six years ago on a star-strewn evening in Leningrad. Surely, if she had answered in his favor, things might have turned out differently. For all of them.

"I don't know how to thank you, Aranoff."

His gaze roamed her face. She saw that long ago evening in the back of his eyes, recognized the hurt, the resignation. Her throat tightened. Then he leaned close and kissed her on the forehead. She steeled herself against the rush of emotions and the betraying tears that pricked her eyes. Aranoff would have never betrayed her, and that realization made her ache to her marrow.

"Stay here," he said, the memory erased, now turning his eyes cold. "I'll be right back."

She watched him steal back through the forest, where the traitorous guard waited for his payoff. Aranoff's wide shoulders hunched as he fought the rake of the cold wind, and she wondered if she'd chosen the right man when she married Michael Moore.

"Vastavai!"

The command raked over Mickey's frozen, bruised body and roused him enough to groan.

"Vastavai!"

This time the guard, silhouetted in the outline of the door, strode in and grabbed him by his hair. Mickey scrambled to his feet, the room spinning. Caked blood rimmed his bottom lip, which still felt fat. He stared at the guard, a chill of fear rushing through him.

This was it.

Execution at midnight. He didn't know what the exact time was, but the way the moonlight draped through his window, it felt like the hour of death. He shot a glance upward, feeling a sudden and thorough relief. With him dead, Nadia would be of no use to the KGB. He hadn't quite figured out what they meant when they'd said she was "back." Hadn't she been living in Moscow all this time? Yes, she'd left their apartment on Komsolmosky Boulevard, but he figured she'd moved in with friends. . .probably to make a point—one he should have paid attention to. He'd only begun to make inquiries when he was arrested.

The fact she'd never come to visit him he'd attributed to his abysmal job as a husband, her covert activities, and the plain fact that even he didn't know where he'd been taken. It could be Far East Russia for all he knew. He'd spent the better part of the trip, via boxcar, recuperating from a broken collarbone and a case of the flu.

But maybe their words meant something entirely different. As in, back. . .in Russia?

He felt a hole open in his stomach as his thoughts

ground out the painful truth. She had returned to America. To get their marriage annulled.

"Da," he said, as if agreeing to the next activity, and stumbled forward. His calloused, bare feet felt like dead weight, and he took extra care stepping over the metal threshold. The guard prodded him with the sharp end of his weapon even as Mickey turned and stumbled past Evgeny's cell.

Evgeny sat up, crawled to the door, stuck his hand through. "Be strong, Mickey." His voice sounded thick. " 'Blessed is the man who does not fall away. . . .' "

Mickey nodded, although the shadows swallowed his response.

Die well.

He'd been fighting to stay alive for this moment, to honor his country, his wife. . .even his God in this death. He might not have lived well, but he'd kept his country's secrets, and he somehow felt that was a purpose ordained by the Almighty.

Why else would God allow him to survive through the cold, the beatings, the sickness, the despair?

He lifted his chin, attempted a straight back.

I'm sorry, Nadia.

Longing swept through him, nearly crippling him as he stepped through the door into the outer corridor. Why hadn't he listened to her pleas to stay home? If only she could hear him say one last time, "I love you."

She didn't deserve this.

Or maybe she did. Maybe this was God's retribution for Mickey's disrespect. For marrying Edward's daughter without a glance toward permission or honor. He'd taken what he'd wanted. And Nadia deserved the chance to start over with someone who could honor her, be a faithful husband instead of an accomplished liar.

They descended a barely lit corridor. A musty basement smell drifted up from the dungeons below and tightened his chest.

He'd hoped for a firing squad or a hanging. Weakness rushed through him at the thought of another, final beating.

He felt pretty sure that there wasn't an inch on his body not already bruised. He licked his fat, chapped lip and grabbed the rail.

Die well.

No secrets.

Reaching the bottom of the stairs, he turned as if to continue, but the guard stopped him. He screwed his gun barrel into Mickey's tailbone. "*Prama.*"

Mickey frowned but stumbled forward toward the door. He pulled it open and nearly gasped at the rush of cold air, the breath of night against the pine trees, the stripped poplar and birch. The cruelty of the act clawed his breath out of his chest. Yeah, let him glimpse freedom seconds before snuffing out that freedom in the dank cellars. These Russians knew how to drive suffering home.

Lord, help me. He glanced upward, knowing he wasn't the man he hoped to be. He'd have to have God's courage to meet this moment without crumbling.

He'd wanted so much more for his life.

He'd wanted to accomplish something great. Something eternal.

He nearly choked on his failures.

The guard pushed Mickey across the threshold, making him step onto the cold ground. He barely felt the scrape of weeds against his legs.

"Begee!"

Run?

Mickey half-turned, fury welling up from a place of courage in his chest. *"Nyet!"* They weren't going to shoot him like a dog in a field. If they wanted his life, let them face him, watch the life drain out of him. *"Nyet."*

"Begee!" A blow across his back buckled his knees. As he gasped for breath, he heard the guard fill the chamber of his AK-47. His heartbeat hiccupped, and he looked up, shaking.

"Ya ne bydo egraet stboy!" He wasn't going to play their games, amuse them with his final moments. He wrestled to his feet, propped his hand against the building. The cold wrapped around his chest, raising gooseflesh, but his heart raced, and anger blazed a path through his pain.

The guard stared at him. Mickey tracked back to last night, wondering if this was the new guy. Still, guards seemed to blur when they used their fists for identification. Up close, this one seemed young, and his dark eyes held the etchings of fear. *"Begee,"* he repeated, this time his voice low.

It was the tone that made Mickey blink, his heart stopping a second before it pushed him to flight.

Maybe?

If this was a game, perhaps he could still win.

He bolted, a dangerous euphoria filling his lungs.

The first shot whizzed by him merely ten meters into his escape. He didn't look back, didn't slow. Focusing on the clump of forest that ringed the compound, he felt his pulse and a mounting hope pump adrenaline into his muscles. He had to be running like a lame man, stumbling, tripping over weeds and rocks, tearing the flesh from his numb feet, but as the second shot zinged over his head, he knew he just might have a chance.

Only, what if he made it? An American in prison skivvies just might stand out against the barren landscape. He'd get picked off faster than a peacock in the middle of Siberia.

But within the unknown lay hope.

He balled his fists and dove for the forest.

Tree branches, honed for winter, tore at him as another shot ricocheted off a large pine. He ducked and dragged in ragged, blessed breaths. He felt suddenly, amazingly healed. Powerful.

Free.

He gulped in hope and plowed through the forest without a thought to his battered body or the fresh taste of blood on his lips.

The trees latticed the moonlight as he drove into the darkness. The sounds of shouting, the bark of dogs punctuated the night. His heart plummeted. Now he'd be torn into a million painful pieces by the local Rottweilers.

He fought the claw of panic as he gulped in fiery breaths and aimed for the dent of light on the far side of the trees. If he could make it to the town, he just might find a nice sweet hay mound or potato bin, maybe a clothesline.

Perhaps a kind babushka who might have pity, even mercy.

He parted the arms of a fir and felt the presence behind him in the intake of breath a second before he whirled and met it with a fist. They'd take him down slugging.

"Whoa!" The figure ducked, caught his arm, and had him flipped on his back faster than he could blink. "Mickey, it's me."

Perhaps it was the dark, the cold numbing his reflexes, the adrenaline twisting his brain, or simply his wildest dreams sucking him under. Whatever the case, he couldn't help but believe he saw his Hope in the fading light of consciousness.

CHAPTER FOUR

Despite his year in gulag, with the beatings served daily alongside his wormy kasha and stale brown bread, Mickey still had the power to sweep the breath out of Hope's chest, even without a smile. Anger, frustration, bewilderment, it all worked.

But this expression—the one that questioned if she might be some sort of celestial being—had taken her heart along with it.

How long had she waited to see *that* in his eyes?

"Hope?" His gaze unfocused, and she saw him fight the wave of unconsciousness.

"You got it, baby. It's me. Now get up!" She grabbed his arms, began tugging him to a sitting position. She hadn't meant to body slam him, but she hadn't been prepared for his attack. Short of slapping him, it was the only thing she could think of.

His head rolled, and he blinked, as if trying to clear it.

"Put your arm around me." The barking of manic dogs slashed the air, fighting the rush of wind against the barren trees. Thankfully, the animals sounded disoriented. She hoped the human scent she'd laid to the far edge of the forest had distracted them, pulling them off Mickey's trail. "It's not much farther."

He must be hurting the way he so easily succumbed to

her ministrations. He draped an arm around her, let her grab his waist, and she half-dragged, half-led him through the forest to where her Zhiguli sat, idling. His breath emerged ragged, as if this two-hundred-meter dash to freedom had sucked out his last reserves. She tried to fortify her heart, but she'd gotten a glimpse of his battered face in the fractured moonlight, and even that had the power to spear her in half.

They'd hurt him.

She ground her teeth as she opened the back door and all but pushed him in. "Get down. There's a blanket and some clothes there. Put them on."

She wasn't sure if he heard her, the way he crumpled onto the seat, but she'd dress him later if she had to.

She had been doing that for a year to his little girl.

Ekaterina, I found your daddy. She fought a sudden rush of emotions and climbed into the driver's seat, forced the Zhiguli into gear, and tore out of her secret lair in the forest. She spun onto the road and floored it, kicking up loose gravel, deciding against turning on the headlights. The moonlight, splintered by the cloud cover, strafed the road like the beams of a border patrol, and she swerved around the light lest it glint off her car like a neon "Here I am, come get me!" sign.

"Mickey, are you okay?"

Nothing. No grunt. No sigh. Her throat tightened. "Mickey?"

She glanced behind. He was curled on the seat in the fetal position, teeth chattering.

Anger felt like a hot pool of lava in her gut. The guy had no shoes, no shirt. What had they done to him in there? A spurt of tears betrayed her razed nerves, and she took a vicious swipe at them. *Keep it cool, Nadia.* The last thing they needed was for her to freak out. *Be the operator you were taught to be.*

She slowed as she neared town and flicked on the lights. At this late hour, the town slept. Only a few unbroken spotlights betrayed the jail breakers. Pulling into a side street, she again popped off the lights, wound down another street, then rolled into a grassy, abandoned enclave between two metal garages.

She turned the car off and heard nothing but her roaring heartbeat. And Mickey's chattering teeth.

Thank You, God. She looked heavenward and let the emotions of the moment pile against her, thickening her chest. She'd done it—launched them into a new era. An era of faith. Of family. She'd never considered herself wise, had somehow always valued guts over prudence. But these last two years without Mickey to steady her had made her realize how much she had relied on his faith to keep her grounded. She'd grown up steeped in the religious teaching of her grandmother, but it wasn't until she'd become a mother herself that she realized that faith wasn't inherited. It had to be taught. And somehow, the key to all that was locked in a gulag in Siberia. Life without Mickey in the background, shouting wisdom and words of caution, left her feeling naked. Alone. Cold.

More than anything, she longed for the warmth of his love, and she hoped she was right to follow her gut feeling to trust him, despite the rumors.

Climbing over the seat, she landed next to him, and for a moment, her heart lodged in the middle of her throat and silenced her. *Mickey. Her Mickey. Shivering.*

She wanted to cry at what they'd done to him. She

grabbed the blanket Aranoff had scrounged up and tucked it over him. "Mickey, you gotta stay awake." She crouched next to him, and he opened his eyes.

Light green and beautiful. Wise. Strong. "Am I dead?"

She touched his temple, traced her finger down the side of his cheek where it turned into scraggly brown beard. "Nope."

" 'Cause I feel dead."

"You're just cold. You'll be warm in a minute."

"Is it you?"

She smiled, nodded, longing moving through her, awakening from some eternal hibernation. "Yes. I couldn't let them kill you."

His hair had grown past his shoulders, a wavy, matted mop. He'd fit right in to the hippie movement in the States and be horrified. Mickey had done enough time in Vietnam before the war hit full stride to cultivate a soul-deep dislike for war protesters, even if he would give his life for world peace.

But today, arm him with a love van and a psychedelic T-shirt and he'd look like Bob Dylan.

"You'll be fine, I promise. We just gotta get you out of this country and safely home," she soothed.

"We?" He swallowed, his Adam's apple moving in his throat.

Her pulse skipped. "I. We, as in you and me."

He reached up, caught her hand as it moved through his beard. He stared at her as he pressed her palm to his lips. "I'm not sure if I should hug you or strangle you."

Strangle me? She slowly pulled her hand away. "Glad to see you, too."

He opened his mouth, as if only realizing his words, and

something sparked in his eyes. Something hot. . .and just dangerous enough to send through her a rush of fear. Yes, buried under all the hair, the grime, the bruises, her Mickey, the guy who fought her for the last word, still lived.

His eyes hardened, and he pushed himself to a sitting position. He clenched his jaw, as if holding back pain, and as the moonlight illuminated his face, she got a good look at the scars he'd earned. His fattened lower lip had bled out into his beard, and the faintest tracings of a black eye outlined his cheek. She slid back onto the seat and brushed her gaze over him. He'd thinned considerably, but the outline of rangy muscle remained on his arms and chest, giving him a lean, even dangerous aura. With the blanket around his shoulders like a cape, she could only make out a very nasty bruise on his left side. She cringed and reached out to touch it.

He jerked away, eyes on her. "Did you say clothes?"

Her throat tightened as she shifted to find the clothes Aranoff had left for him. Aranoff, her *kind* friend, the one who had scooped her up in a bone-crunching, enthusiastic hug the moment he saw her. She tried not to let it sting that Mickey wasn't thrilled to see her. Couldn't he be just a bit happy to be. . .rescued? From death?

She gathered up the pants, shirt, jacket, and shoes. "They might not be that clean."

He huffed a short burst of apathy. "Clean is relative."

She nearly threw the clothes at him. "Fine. Make it snappy. We have a train to catch in Kisligorsk."

She turned away and crossed her arms over her chest, fighting a swell of grief as he shucked on the wool pants, the gray flannel shirt, and the green army jacket. With a little makeup and a rabbit *shopka,* he'd look like a fifty-year-old factory worker traveling to Moscow with his trendy daughter. Where said daughter would exchange their disguises for that of aid workers and smuggle them across the border into Finland.

If Mickey didn't decide to hightail it back to the woman he loved first. Lena Chornova. The rumors suddenly felt heartbreakingly true.

"I am glad to see you, Nadia. I'm just. . .surprised." Mickey laced the old leather boots, tied them less than nimbly with what looked like calloused, stiff fingers. She wanted to weep at his pain.

"Obviously."

He touched her on the shoulder, his hand both gentle and firm. "Nadia. . .I'm. . .let's just get out of here, okay?"

She shrugged away his touch, feeling suddenly tired, so tired she just wanted to curl in a ball and sob. "Yeah. Don't worry. I'll get you back to Moscow as fast as I can." *Back to your mistress.*

She got out, stalked around the car, climbed in the front seat, and fired up the engine. "Keep down. We gotta be in Kisligorsk by dawn."

He hadn't meant to offend her.

He watched his wife drive him to safety, to freedom, and felt like a dog. Worse, he wished the KGB had finished the job during his sprint into the woods. Then she wouldn't be risking her beautiful neck for him, the man who was supposed to honor and protect her. But she'd lived up to her name, Crazy Hope. And now, they had the KGB tracking them like hounds on a rabbit. With any luck, they'd die in a shootout and not limb by mangled limb.

His worst nightmares had just gone from monochrome to Technicolor. If Nadia was in trouble before, she was surely a goner after this stunt.

"Nadia—"

"Go to sleep, Mickey. You look terrible. You need your rest." (As opposed to her.) He couldn't imagine what she'd been through to save him. . .he'd barely been able to get past his disbelief, his sheer euphoria to find words to grasp that his Hope had returned for him.

He loved her so much it made him ache. Instead of telling her that, however, he'd erupted in typical Mickey style when faced with his greatest fears. He'd let his arrogant mouth protect his heart and emerged with something stupid. He just couldn't—despite his mind-blowing joy—ignore the idea that he was her death sentence.

Edward's predictions were one firing squad shot away from coming true.

She looked more beautiful than he'd remembered. Ever. Even in his deepest, most delicious dreams in gulag. She wore a stocking cap that perfectly framed her high, regal cheekbones and wide, golden brown eyes, and the sight of her had knocked him. . .well, he was still trembling. And something about her. She seemed. . .steadier.

She'd touched him, actually put her incredibly soft hands, those elegant fingers into his filthy beard, and he'd only felt disgust that he'd dragged her into his nightmare. Not glad to see her? He'd only conjured up this moment for over a year, actually practiced his apologies if the moment ever materialized. And when it did, all he could do was stare. And then threaten to strangle her.

What a hero.

Even better. Husband of the Year. He should win

awards.

He wanted to leap the seat, pull her into his arms, and kiss her. Remind her of the love that had kept him alive, that had been his very breath. Remind her of everything they'd had.

Had.

Oh yeah. Maybe she wasn't his anymore. A ball of grief stopped up his throat, and he had to swallow it down. Then why had she returned to spring him?

Maybe she was on assignment. *I couldn't let them kill you.* Not, *I love you.* Big difference. Yes, definitely on duty.

Which would account for the cold shoulder. The crisp tones. The way the car felt glacial despite the heat pouring from the ducts.

Fine. They'd get back to Moscow, and then he'd make sure she got kicked out of the country. And fast. He still had some pull. At least, he hoped he did. Thirteen months of gritting his teeth for the company as the KGB knocked the stuffing out of him should merit him a few favors, right?

"I'm not tired," he said in response to her curt order. That was the understatement of the year. He was so not tired he thought he might be able to run all the way to Moscow. Yes, deep inside, his bones were exhausted, the kind of fatigue that made him want to curl into a ball and surrender. But this sudden turn of events, i.e., freedom, felt like a shot of pure adrenaline. On this high, he could go full tilt until he got Nadia out of Russia.

Maybe even until he found the man who betrayed him.

Or was it a woman?

Someone had set him up, told the KGB where to find Aranoff's safe house. He still shivered at the memory of awaking to find the cold, blunt end of a Makarov pistol shoved into his trachea.

Thankfully, he'd had the wisdom to send the proof of his patriotism, and value, to a post office box in Moscow for Nadia to retrieve. And she, like a wise spy, found his pictures, the plans, and sent warnings to the right people about the upcoming RORSAT launch. His teeth ground at the thought of the Russians tracking the US Navy's every move.

He glanced at her, at the set of her jaw, the way the moonlight caressed her noble features and felt old emotions burst to life inside him. Mickey and Nadia together again. It was enough to push the envelope of surreal and send him back two years into the cradle of his wildest dreams.

Oh, he'd missed her. "You look. . .good."

Please tell me you found the postcards!

She didn't glance at him, but when she shook her head in disgust, his heart fell. "Yeah, I'm Miss America. Go to sleep, Mickey."

Ouch. Okay, yes, he'd hurt her. "You look different. Did you cut your hair?"

She looked at him, and he saw words in her eyes, then she closed her mouth. "Yeah, that's it. I cut my hair." She shook her head and turned her eyes back to the road, and he felt like a gutter rat. Obviously, he still had that Mickey Moore wind-the-girls-around-his-little-finger charm.

He slumped in his seat, watching the landscape slide by. She drove like a maniac, swerving around ruts, hitting enough of them to jar the teeth right out of his skull. He braced one arm on the ceiling, the other on the door. "Slow down."

"I'm driving here. You just. . ." She bit off her words,

and he wondered at her unfinished sentence.

He leaned forward, his old frustration rising like a bear out of hibernation. "Slow down, woman. You're going to leave our axles in the dirt, and then where will we be?"

"I got you this far, Jack. Somehow I'll figure out the rest."

Her knuckles were white on the steering wheel. He fought the growl forming in his chest. Crazy Hope. Always pushing one step ahead of wisdom. Only problem, she usually accomplished her mission. . .without being arrested and tortured.

Still, there was always a first time. He muscled his way over the front seat and sat down opposite her. The dash light illuminated her jaw, now tight, and turned her eyes to gold.

"Go back in the back."

"No. Let me drive."

She looked at him with an expression that reminded him painfully of a sassy student he'd met ten years ago. "Not on your life."

He crossed his arms and leaned back, watching the moonlight scrape the fields. "Where are we?"

"South of Leningrad about two hours."

"I thought I might be in Siberia."

Silence.

"I feared I was never going to see you again."

She sighed. Swallowed.

"I am glad to see you, Hope."

"So glad you'd like to strangle me?"

As a matter of fact, yes. Right after I kiss you. Oh, she'd like that. Especially with him looking—and smelling—his current scumbag best. His erratic emotions tied his brain into a knot, so he said nothing and looked out the window.

If he had any doubts that this beautiful agent dressed in a field brown jacket and stocking cap was his Hope, his knotted gut told the truth. Yes, this was his Hope, his Nadia, the one who could turn him inside out with a smile, knock him flat on his back with a scowl.

The one who still trusted him? Doubtful.

"I just don't want you to get hurt," he added.

She pursed her lips in that irritating way that always made him want to duck. "Well, I guess you should have thought about my feelings two years ago."

He flinched at her words. She'd definitely moved on. Found someone else to fill her life. He closed his eyes and heard something inside him howl. It died to a low murmur, a soft voice spoken from the edges of his childhood. *"Who can find a virtuous woman? For her price is far above rubies. The heart of her husband doth safely trust in her, so that he shall have no need of spoil. She will do him good and not evil all the days of her life."*

He put a hand to his chest, his warm, *clothed* chest, and knew he so didn't deserve this woman. "Thanks for rescuing me, Nadia."

She sighed, and when he glanced over, her eyes glistened. *"Nyet problema."*

CHAPTER FIVE

The morning sun boiled off the fog that crept across the Kisligorsk train platform. Nadia stalked toward the dingy white Zhiguli, a loaf of brown bread in one hand, a bottle of vodka in the other. The trappings of Russian peasantry. Tucking the bottle under her arm, she opened the door, then slid in beside Mickey.

He eyed her with the gaunt, edgy look of a man on the lam. Stealing herself against a tug toward mercy, something probably inherent to her recent stride into motherhood, she handed him the bread. "Breakfast."

"And that?" He nodded toward the clear bottle with the red label.

"Part of your disguise."

He made a face, then tore the bread into two halves. He still had strong hands, but she saw they were reddened, chapped. He handed her half. "Thanks."

"Just pretend it's a steak. Or better yet, turkey dinner." She resisted the urge to rub her fingers gently on the bruise under his eye, as if ascertaining that it really was Mickey under all that hair and hurt. She tore off a chunk of the earthy, molasses-tasting bread and chewed it down.

"I don't remember the last time I had a turkey dinner," he said quietly as he looked out the window. Pigeons braving the early November cold pecked at sunflower shells scattered in the frozen mud beside the depot. An unruly wind tossed crisp brown leaves into the air and threw them at their windshield. She heard the garbled announcement of an incoming train and reached inside her jacket for her watch.

"You still have it." His gaze landed on the gift, and behind his eyes, she saw him peel back time to their honeymoon. For a second, she joined him in the past. Saw him emerge dripping wet and handsome from the hot springs behind their secluded cabin in the Black Forest. He wore a sly smile, one that always had the power to send a hot ripple to her toes. He wrapped a towel around his swimsuit as he sauntered toward her. "I left something in your robe." She'd been reading something by Kafka, her author of the moment, and settled the book open on her chest. He sat next to her on the chaise lounge, the sun behind his head casting his expression into shadow. "Check your pocket."

She'd pulled out the timepiece. He'd shown her the secret compartment in back, one that already contained a microdot note. "But I can't read it," she'd protested.

He leaned close, his masculine fragrance thick and so calming. "You don't have to. It's a picture of you and me at the embassy party." She remembered now, just as she had then, the significance of that event. "It's a reminder." He traced one long finger down her cheekbone. "When things aren't as they seem, you alone have the truth."

What his cryptic words meant, she had no idea, but later she took them as a sort of prophecy. Or defense. As if he'd known she'd discover his adulterous liaisons.

She tucked the watch back into her shirt. "How are you feeling this morning?"

He swallowed, as if knowing she'd dodged his unspoken question—do you still trust me?—and looked away. Why did she suddenly feel like the two-timing dog?

"I'm okay. A little stiff." He took another bite, not acting for a moment like a man who'd been denied a thousand or so meals. He glanced at her. "You must be tired."

"A little." Her neck screamed, and she'd gladly pay another five thousand smackerels for a hot shower and a decent bed. "I'm going to change clothes, so I need you to look the other way."

He eyed her, one eyebrow up, a smile nudging up his cheek. "Nadezhda, c'mon, do you think I don't remember what you look like?"

Her cheeks burned, and she narrowed her eyes at him. "Listen, Mickey, I know what you were up to in Moscow after you supposedly left, so you're lucky I don't just leave you behind as Rottweiler fodder. Turn. Around."

His smile vanished; his face paled. He turned, muttering.

She shucked off the pants, pulled on her dingy skirt from the nightclub. Thankfully, they'd parked under the cover of a large oak, its shadow obscuring the car from wandering eyes. She zipped up her black boots, then shook out her hair, piled it atop her head, and snuggled on the black wig. She felt smelly and grimy and about the furthest thing from a hip college girl. But she'd add a swing to her stride, and with a little more divine intervention, they'd make it on the train.

"Okay, I'm done."

He turned back, and the expression on his face turned her warm from the inside. "You look. . .good."

"Don't get any ideas, Mickey. I'm not the girl you left behind."

His face twitched, and that hurt expression passed across it. “Yeah. I guess not.”

Now what did he mean by that? She glared at him. “Finish eating. The train is about to pull in.”

She saw questions forming in his eyes. He opened his mouth, then closed it and turned back to the window.

She balled her hands on the seat. Why had he married her if he only intended to make a mockery of their marriage? For power? Position? Had he thought that Edward would change his opinion of Mickey after he slid a ring on Nadia’s finger? Perhaps he believed as the husband of Edward Neumann’s daughter he’d have the ear of one of the most powerful men in Europe.

That assumption proved horribly erroneous the moment he’d been thrown into the clink. She clenched her jaw at her father’s hard-hearted reaction. *“I told you he was trouble.”*

Mistake, Mistake, Mistake.

Still, he wore the scars of a man who had toughed it out for his country. A die-hard patriot. Maybe he hadn’t double-crossed their love. Maybe, in fact, she should ignore the rumors of his adultery, just as she had repulsed the reports of his betrayal.

“You know, Mickey, no one would blame you if you had folded in there.” She watched his jaw tighten, the Adam’s apple bob in his throat.

“Yeah, well, I didn’t.” He suddenly looked about a million years old, worn, defeated. His eyes devoid of the spark that had lit them from the inside. *Oh Mickey, what did they do to you?*

She couldn’t bear to pursue the rumors.

They ate in silence, watching the train churn into the station. “It’s time, Mickey,” she said as the train coughed out black exhaust. "Ready?" She used the dashboard to pop off the vodka cover like she might a bottle of Coca-Cola.

He visibly reeled from the smell. "You're not. . .I don't have to drink that. . .right?"

"Nope. Just smell like it." She waggled her eyebrows in warning a second before she shook the vodka onto his jacket, his pants. The odor swilled the car, driving them out.

The sunshine felt like a balm on her face, and the smell of autumn rode the air, despite the redolence of coal smoke and dust churned up by the train. *"Da'vai, Peonitz,"* she said, calling him by the Russian nickname for drunkard. He glared at her, but did she see the slightest etching of challenge in his eyes?

Uh-oh. It ignited all the old feelings, the ones that included Nadia and Mickey, the Cold War couple, the unstoppable duo who danced through danger.

Please, no. She couldn't start enjoying his company. Not when her heart felt so fragile, so easily duped. She couldn't give into the nudge to love him, to hand him her heart if he was only going to decimate it. She pulled her leather bag—traded at the market for her backpack—over her shoulder and stalked toward the train.

He held the vodka bottle in one hand and began a half-shuffle, half-swagger behind her.

She hadn't gone three meters when she heard, in a voice that sounded too much like Russian bluster, *"Dochka! Po-dosh-di!"*

No, she wasn't going to wait for him. She turned, scowled. Oh yeah, he wanted to play. *"Poshli!"* she ground out, acting the impatient daughter. "I'm not going to be late for university this time."

A babushka rushed by towing her grandson by a white

grip and nodded to Nadia. Nadia didn't smile, guarding against a sure foreign tell. *"Bwestra!"* she hollered, backing up, as if reeling him in.

Mickey took a mock swig from the bottle, then wiped his chin and stumbled toward her. Or was that a controlled swagger? She rolled her eyes, hooked her arm into his, and prodded him across the outdoor platform. When she arrived at the steps, she handed the conductor her ticket with a deep sigh.

"Please forgive my father," she said in annoyed Russian. "He's still celebrating his birthday."

The woman, pushing back the retirement look with dyed carrot red hair and a wide, burly face, glanced at him and shoved the ticket back at Nadia. Nadia practically pulled the joker onto the day train, tripping with him down the skinny aisle to their berth.

Thank you, Aranoff, for purchasing for us one of the rare, and expensive, private coupee *berths.* She half-threw Mickey onto the leather seat, slammed the sliding door, and locked it.

He was grinning when she turned. "Oh, very funny, Mickey. As if we didn't have the KGB breathing down our necks."

"You wanted me to be convincing." He lifted the bottle, as if to bring it to his lips, and she swiped it out of his hand. "Testy this morning?"

She glared at him. "I have one goal." She lifted her index finger. "Get you to Moscow, pick up the plane ticket one of our operatives left in our PO box, then get you home."

His smile fell. "Our PO box? Did you. . .pick up anything from there? Is it empty?"

She frowned at him. "No. I haven't. . .well, no, Mickey,

I didn't stop by to check the mail on my way to sneak into Gilorsk to break you out of jail. I'm sorry. Were you expecting something? Fan mail, perhaps?" She didn't know why but she felt about two seconds short of snapping.

"Sit down, Nadia."

She stared at him, seeing past the tangled beard, the bruised eyes, the fat lip to the man who could, and had, defended himself against five KGB agents in a fight. The man whose brain always ticked, like a time bomb. The man who had a wise saying for every occasion and who, despite her father's decree, braved expulsion and the disintegration of his career to love her.

Or at least convince her that he loved her. That thought tore into the soft flesh of her heart. After his brutal confirmation this morning—the one where he proved he was less than happy to see her—she thought she might be, finally, immune to his powers. A wise girl would plug her ears, close her eyes, and run from temptation.

She sat. Crossed her arms. "What?"

He leaned on his knees and rubbed the back of his neck. "You didn't get any mail in the PO box? Nothing? No postcards? No letters?"

"No. Why? Did you send me something?"

He huffed, a short burst of incredulity. "I sent you. . ." He closed his eyes against some unknown pain. "Never mind."

Never mind? After she'd just saved him from a firing squad? She glared at him. "Spill it, Mickey. I have a right to know. What did you send me? A Dear John letter? Or maybe something addressed to Lena? Did you perhaps want me to play postmistress? Oh, wait, I forgot, you already have a mistress."

His eyes widened, and his jaw actually dropped, as if her discovery of his misdeeds shocked him. As if he believed that she wouldn't find out. She had her sources, too. She hadn't been a very accomplished spook for nearly a decade without cultivating her own "friends."

The snake.

Realizing that he hadn't denied her accusations, just looked horrified that he'd been discovered, she gave a huff of pure anger and stared out the window.

Where she saw a small contingency of KGB regulars, complete with black leather jackets and Makarovs in their pockets, in a pregame huddle. Backdropped by the morning sun, they resembled a group of hunchback beetles. The sight raised the tiny hairs on the back of her neck.

"Uh, we have trouble."

Mickey turned, looked out the window. Took a deep breath. "They're not after you, yet. Maybe I should just surrender."

What? Her disbelief must have shown on her face, for he sat back, actually grimaced, and had the audacity to look sorry under all that hair.

"Not on your life, Jack." She reached into her pocket and pulled out a flashlight. Inside it was concealed a 4.5 mm firing device. Not much against a small armada of dedicated professionals, but she'd hide out in the hallway, surprise them, maybe give Mickey time to run.

His green eyes widened. "No, Nadia. I'm not worth it."

She didn't argue. Not anymore. "Stay put."

He grabbed her arm as she started for the door. "I am serious. I'm not letting you put your life on the line for me."

She felt the anger spiral out of her and couldn't reel it

back in. Yanking out of his grasp, she rounded on him. "You know, you're absolutely right. I should just let them march in here and shoot you at dawn. But some foolish part inside me can't ignore the fact that I said yes to the ' 'til death do you part' section in our vows, and one of us needs to keep her promises! Especially for—"

She clamped her renegade mouth shut a second before Ekaterina's name could pop out. Oh, where was the better part of wisdom—silence—when she needed it? Why had she rushed back to the Soviet Union like a lovesick puppy to put her life on the line for a husband who didn't love her? The idiocy of her own actions sent a tremble through her. Maybe she should just let them come and get the jerk. Ditch him while she still had the chance.

Except, wouldn't that make her just like him? A betrayer. An adulterer to their commitment. She couldn't believe she'd actually spent the last year wooing herself into believing his innocence. She'd told her common sense that he was a *spy,* after all. A man who made his living by peddling a dual life. She'd done a first-class job of convincing herself that the rumors about Lena had been nothing more than window dressing, part of the ruse to hide their relationship of handler-agent. She'd even taken steps toward desperation and called his actions "duty." It felt like a flimsy foothold, at best, but she had planted that thought in her brain and let it flourish.

She told herself it wouldn't matter anyway. They would return to America. To a new start. And she'd make him forget all about the double life he'd led.

What a fool she'd been. If they wriggled out of this mess, she'd gift wrap him and drop him off on Lena's doorstep. So much for him pining away in the darkest, coldest hours in gulag, dreaming of his Hope.

Perilously close to tears, she reached for the door, her weapon in her fist.

The train lurched, a jolt that then eased into movement. She whirled and stared out the window. The KGB contingency now milled around the platform like a surveillance crew. As if waiting for their prey to arrive. . .or perhaps disembark? It pricked her already buzzing suspicions, and she frowned at their actions as the train rolled forward.

"You don't think. . ."

Mickey, too, stared at the activity, and she saw confusion in his eyes. "It's almost like they know we're here."

"Maybe they're not after us."

He gave her a look that was 100 percent seasoned spy.

"Okay, so why would they let us go?"

He swallowed, sat down, and his shoulders hunched. "Maybe they want us on this train."

His conclusion, spoken so softly so as nearly not to be heard, made her tremble.

Mickey watched her fall back on the seat, frown, stare out the window, her brain unsnarling his words, fixing them into place, and spitting out a solution.

The way she thought on her feet frightened him more than he wanted to admit. Half adrenaline, half dare, she managed to get them into—and out of—more scrapes than he could count.

Crazy Hope.

He touched her on her knee, repulsed by his own odor, drawn in by hers. She had an air of regality about her that notched up his pulse and made her always seem just a tad too perfect. Especially for a guy like him.

The princess and the peasant from Canton, Ohio. The comparison, so close to the one Edward had made, stung.

"Keep away from her, Michael. You'll only hurt her." Edward Neumann, Super Spy, the master of controllers, and most importantly, Michael's boss, had backed him into a corner, his finger against Michael's collarbone. "She doesn't need a playboy with a trigger finger for adventure messing with her heart. Keep your distance." The *clack-clack-clack* of the train on the well-traveled rails pounded the indictments farther into his thoughts.

Oh, the arrogance of his youth. Michael had actually lifted his chin and glared at the man. As if Edward couldn't send him packing back to the States and demote him to pushing a broom around the bathrooms of the Pentagon.

As if to illustrate his arrogance, Michael had brushed past the guy and straight out onto the dance floor, where he cut in on Nadia, dancing with Aranoff. He hadn't missed the dark look that sparked in Aranoff's eyes, but he chose to ignore it.

She fit perfectly in Michael's arms, just as he'd imagined—and hoped. She curled her fingers around his neck, into the collar of his tuxedo. Around them, the murmur of embassy officials and foreigners, mixing it up with official Russians, hummed under the Strauss waltz, but Mickey ignored it and buried his gaze in Nadia's beautiful face.

She smiled. "Mickey, I wonder if your mind is on our job or perhaps on something else?"

She waggled her thin, plucked eyebrows at him, and he could feel his brain start to tangle. He lost himself in her playful tone. "Oh, a little of both, *Nadezhda.*" He winked at her, mostly to keep up with her tease, but it gave him a second to tuck his heart back into his chest. This woman had the uncanny ability to see right through him to the real Mickey Moore.

A scary prospect for a guy who made his living by lying.

Only, perhaps deep inside the layers of deception, he hoped she might uncover the truth. That he was falling terribly in love with his favorite operative.

Edward's warning tugged in his mind as he twirled her around the floor. The chandelier's light glinted off the decadence of the New Year tree, trimmed according to Soviet tradition with its bright red lights and the red and silver star at the top. Around the room, glasses tinkled as waiters carried in champagne for the upcoming golden hour. 1964. He leaned close to that tender place right below her ear and whispered as he drew his lips across her neck, "Is the subject in pocket?"

"Lena has him wound around her fingers as we speak," she replied, also under her breath. Did he imagine it, or did her voice shake?

He searched the room for his double agent. Lena Chornova had, more than once, proven her loyalty. A ballerina turned director, who relished being the toast of Moscow. She knew how to weave her way into social gatherings and onto the dance cards of the most influential men. Tonight, the blond had the attention of General Pashov. And she'd keep it long enough for Michael and Nadia to sneak into his upstairs office, to plant a bug, and unearth what they hoped might be a list of Russian moles in the CIA. Something too many agents had given their life to obtain.

"Ready?"

Without a glance toward Edward, now leaning against the door to the ballroom, they separated, then moseyed upstairs: Nadia through the service entrance; he out the bathroom, up the outside of the building, and through the window she'd opened on the third floor. Her cheeks were flushed. "Hurry."

He climbed over the sill, and she closed the window.

The silence of the office enclosed them, and he felt only the static of his adrenaline and the rush of her soft breath. The place oozed power with the mahogany desk; the carpet turned blood red under the high streetlights; the faces of Lenin, Stalin, and Khrushchev staring from the walls. A velvet sofa and chairs flanked the far wall. The office was big enough to hold the next winter Olympics, with room to spare.

"Do you have the gun?" he asked and moved over to the safe, tucked behind a picture of V. I. Lenin. The wall safe had a pin-and-tumbler lock.

She lifted the folds of that incredibly soft, tastefully body-hugging, eggshell blue dress and extracted a lock pick gun from a sheath strapped to her calf.

He fought the swell of his pulse in his ears as he focused on the lock, listening to the pick strike the pins that worked the locking mechanism. He used a tension wrench to turn the lock cylinder when the pins were properly aligned, and the sound of success was a click no louder than the snap of fingers.

"Bravo," Nadia said, stationed at the door. The music from downstairs filtered up through the winding staircase. Another waltz, this time upbeat. He imagined Nadia nestled back in his arms as he opened the safe and extracted the papers.

"Hurry."

He ignored her, flipped through the stack, his hands steady. He extracted his Minox and began shooting. He'd let the analysts in Washington unravel the secret meanings inside Pashov's safe.

Mickey looked up when Nadia shut the door with a near silent click. "Someone's coming."

She crossed the room in three strides, scooped up the papers, and with a quick flick, tucked them into the safe. She closed the safe and picture in a graceful movement, turned and hooked his arm.

He already had the wardrobe door open, and he pulled her in next to him, concealing them inside just as the office door opened.

Huddled beneath the fur coats, the smell of mothballs filled his nose, and he stifled a sneeze. Nadia's hand cupped his mouth, and he could imagine her beautiful golden brown eyes wide, a finger to her lips. He nodded and listened to the muffled sounds.

Nadia pushed her eye up to the crack in the door. He felt her tense. "Lashtoff," she whispered, and suddenly memory whisked him further back to a train from Moscow to Leningrad, a tiny bathroom, and the still raw feeling of panic. Nadia never had unlocked the events of what had happened two years ago on the train, but the spurts of fear that laced her eyes at the mention of Lashtoff's name, even now as he watched her survey the room, left him wanting to hurt someone. He wasn't sure if he should start with himself, or Colonel, now General Lashtoff.

What was Lashtoff doing in Pashov's office? The question hovered like the smell of mothballs between them. Mickey couldn't deny that the general had some sort of fixation, a vendetta against Oleg Rustikoff's contacts still embedded in Russian culture. But did that determination to root out the sleepers and agents working for the CIA push him to break into a superior's office?

Nadia chronicled his movements in low tones as he opened Pashov's safe, removed the documents, rifled through them, and extracted a file. He left moments later, clicking the door behind, and Nadia let out a long, low breath. "Did you get a picture of that file?"

"I don't know." Mickey's heart sank. "What was he after?"

"I have a guess, but I'm too sickened to voice it."

"We gotta get out of here." Mickey shifted, and the wardrobe creaked. Nadia slammed her hand into his chest.

"Wait." Did she feel his heart racing under her touch? She made a small fist, crunching his tuxedo in her grip. "Someone's here."

The door opened again. What was this, Grand Central? He held his breath, hoping his heartbeat would take the hint. It wasn't Pashov, and even worse, whoever had escaped to this office didn't have business on their mind. Nadia hung her head, tweaked the door closed. "Groovy," she muttered.

Mercifully, the sounds of a record player—some Russian opera star—offered respite from what could have been a painfully awkward situation.

Nadia removed her hand, shifted quietly, and sat beside him. His feet already burned, and he leaned against the end of the wardrobe, holding his breath when the unit creaked. Sitting in the fetal position would cut off the blood supply to his feet faster than knee garters, so he stretched them out along the sides. Nadia settled between his knees, her hands clasped around her knees.

"This is fun," she whispered.

He imagined her smile. Yes, maybe it was. Locked in a cabinet with Nadia. He could think of worse fates. He found her arm, trailed his fingers down it to her hand, held it. It was soft and warm. Edward's voice sounded in the back of his brain, but he ignored it and lifted her hand to his lips. "If this is what it takes to get you alone, well, it can't be all that terrible," he whispered into her soft ear.

She turned her face toward his, and he could feel her smiling even before she leaned close. "Don't get any fancy ideas, Mickey. We're here to work."

"We're working," he said as he traced his finger down her creamy face, hooked her chin, and lifted her mouth to his. He'd only been dreaming of this moment for two years, and what possessed him to act on those dreams—well, it must have been the mothballs eating at his common sense or perhaps the challenge from her father still taunting in the back of his head. He kissed her gently, cupping her cheek with his hand. She had soft, tender lips, and she trembled slightly as he kissed her. It shocked him, and as he drew away and felt her breath, shallow and just a little afraid on his chin, he suddenly had a terrible, rotten-to-the-core feeling.

Everything he'd surmised about Nadia had been a part of her cover. Maybe, just maybe, inside the spitfire girl who faced danger with a smile, lived a. . .girl. A girl who just might be more vulnerable than she let on. A girl who wasn't made of sass and spunk, one who sometimes, just maybe, second-guessed her decisions. A girl who felt fear, despite her efforts to mask it.

A girl who needed a man like him to protect her.

And it was that slight tremble that had pushed his heart over the edge. He stared at her now in the train compartment as she sat across from him. He noted the way she tightened her hands in her lap, poised at the edge of vulnerability, trying to figure out a way to save him. Determination outlined her elegant face, and the same horrible feeling he'd had in the wardrobe now gutted him and left him gasping.

She'd needed a hero.

Instead, she'd gotten a no-good husband who was going to cost her her life.

"Keep away from her, Michael. You'll only hurt her."

He closed his eyes and wanted to cry.

He, too, had one goal. Get Nadia back to Moscow and shove her on a plane before the KGB caught on to who had masterminded his escape.

Only then would he hightail it to his PO box and pray he found the proof to clear his name.

CHAPTER SIX

The soft click of the closing compartment door roused Nadia from her unconscious slump on the seat. She opened her eyes, blinking against the sudden light, and glanced at the intruder, expecting to find a scruffy, rummy-smelling homeless man.

What she saw formed a scream in her chest.

"Shh. . .it's me." Mickey clamped a hand over her mouth to keep her from jumping. His steady green eyes zeroed into hers, practically pinning her to the seat.

She shook herself free of his hand. "I. . .you look. . ." *Great*. Too great. As in stop her heart, turn her weak, make her want to cry great. "Different."

"That's the point." He stepped back, easing his hand off her mouth, and raised his eyebrows as if testing her.

He'd shaved his beard, yet his lean face with its various bruises gave him the aura of a well-heeled ruffian. His brown hair he'd chopped off Beatles' style, then slicked back, completely ditching the Bob Dylan look. It only made his green eyes a thousand times more magnetic, more intoxicating. She heard warning sirens blaring in the common-sense part of her brain. Where had he dug up the black dress pants, matching shoes. . .and was that a state-issued Russian militia shirt? She didn't want to ask. But he smelled. . .like a man. He even had clean breath and aftershave—a powerful and very, very dangerous influence in her fatigued condition.

"You. . .ah. . .still clean up well." Okay, that was the sum of the compliments she would dish out. Especially if she hoped to escape Russia with her heart intact. The guy. . .well, it just wasn't fair that he'd spent a year in gulag and still looked like he could scoop any woman's heart out of her chest with a smile. She stomped down a flare of jealousy.

"Thank you. I was weary of the scumbag look. Besides, they're expecting an escapee with the aura of desperation." He gave her a wry smile. Despite the brisk appearance, he still wore the etchings of chagrin on his expression. She couldn't quite figure out why. . .unless it had something to do with her still-as-yet undenied accusation of his having a mistress.

Or. . .perhaps he had deeper secrets to hide. Ones involving dead agents and information surrendered. Ones that might make him want to hide from his own people when they exited the train.

"Okay, I gotta ask," she said, trying to steer clear of her misgivings. "Where did you get the duds?"

He smiled, pure Mickey, and all the old emotions rushed through her like a spark along a live wire. *No, don't jump start my heart, please.* "He was just coming out of the bathroom. Poor guy. . .when he wakes up he's going to wonder how much he had to drink, and if it has anything to do with the bump on his head."

She grimaced and shook her head, amazed at his resourcefulness. While she'd been conked out against the glass, he'd been plotting their—*his*—escape. She felt like a fool.

Only, she had gotten them this far, hadn't she?

Unless, of course, it hadn't been her. . .but rather a KGB plot from the beginning. She frowned at her thought. No, that would mean that Aranoff helmed a double cross. And why? They had Mickey in their grip, and they still hadn't extracted the information they wanted, right? Or had they?

She rubbed her hand across her forehead, feeling her brain knot. "Okay, what's the plan?"

Outside, the landscape had turned jeweled as they traveled south, the oak and maples clothed in the regal robes of fall. They were drawing closer to Moscow, evidenced by the clumps of dachaville-garden plots with small huts on the property. She noticed a few pensioners gathering the dying harvest as the train rumbled past their yards.

"I'm not going to take the chance of having them pick you up. I think we should head right for the embassy," he said.

His voice, so sure, held none of the pain from last night. The panic, the disbelief, even the harshness had vanished. She looked back at him, at the way he'd slicked back his hair, his fading bruises, the gleam in his eye that hinted at adventure, and realized her old Mickey had returned.

Oh, no.

She sucked a deep breath. If the old Mickey had resurfaced. . .had his ambitions been resurrected along with it? She'd been holding onto the hope that, once beaten, he might relent, surrender to her urges to quit the company, and come home. To her. To Ekaterina.

Only, he hadn't even asked about his daughter—not that he knew he had one, but he had known about her pregnancy, right? Over the past eighteen hours, Nadia's

confidence had plunged to new depths.

What if he didn't want her, even with Ekaterina? Or because of Ekaterina?

Then again, if he wasn't the kind of man who would step up to the plate and be the father her daughter needed. . . well, maybe he could just stay in Russia.

"Marriage? Nadia, what were you thinking? Marriage is for keeps!" Her father's voice, desperate, incredulous, rang behind her ears, and she cringed.

"Are you okay?" Mickey frowned at her.

She sucked in a breath, forced a smile. "Of course. And I'm glad you're thinking the same thing I am. An all-out run for the border."

His face darkened. He licked his lips, then looked out the window. "No, I'm staying here."

Just like that, her last thread of hope snapped. So much for believing that he'd betrayed her for the sake of his country. For believing he still loved her. That maybe, by her tramping into Russia to save him, she might prove her love, her faithfulness, and convince him to return, if not earn his respect. So much for her hope that they might start over, rebuild something stronger from the fragments of their marriage.

"Staying here?" She recoiled as if she'd been slapped. Then, oh no, her face began to crumple. She fought the wave of pain, but it erupted in a horrifying sob. She clamped her hand over her mouth and turned away. "I'm sorry." What a fool, an idealistic dimwit, to think he'd follow her home.

If she even made it home. *Lord, what have I done?*

"Nadia?" His voice, softened, only added sting to her wounds.

She closed her eyes, leaned her head on the cold window, and fought her shaking shoulders.

"Nadia," he repeated, and this time, he kneeled before her. *Get away!*

"Baby, you can't stay here. You've already risked your life enough for me. I can't. . .I won't let you get killed."

She shook her head, unable to find words at his betrayal.

His hands pressed her shoulders; she shrugged away. "Please, Nadia. Can you understand I have to—"

"What? Go back to her?" She winced, furious at her mouth for once again blurting out the truth. How pathetic did she want to seem? But she *was* pathetic. . .she'd risked her life, snuck back into Russia—to save a man who didn't want her.

She'd reached new heights in foolishness.

Fury streaked across his face. "If you're talking about Lena. . .it's not what it looks like."

She slapped him, hard.

He didn't even recoil, and she felt even sicker. Hadn't he had enough beatings over the past year? Still, the rat deserved her punishment. Her face crumpled again, and she wound her hands around her waist. "Get away from me."

His expression hardened. "You listen to me. Whatever they told you—whatever your dad told you—it isn't true. Nadia, I never, ever betrayed you. I. . ." His gaze roamed her face a second before his expression washed with agony, a deep soul-gripping pain that she felt deep in her chest. "Baby, I love you. Enough to send you home for your own good."

His gaze stopped on her mouth, lingered as if debating. Then he reached for her. He kissed her hard. Hungrily. He wrapped his arms around her and pulled her into his chest and kissed her like he had in the wardrobe in General Pashov's office, inside the shadows of the Bolshoi Theater, and every night of their honeymoon. She tried to resist, tried not to put her arms around him and lose herself in the memory of his love. But Mickey had a magic in his touch that she could never resist. And the way he was kissing her, as if he'd really, truly missed her. . .

She kissed him back, letting herself believe in everything she'd longed for.

"Oh Mickey, I've missed you," she whispered. "This is why I came back. For us."

He pulled away, but instead of love, fear etched his face. "Came back?"

"To Russia." Why did he look like he'd been slapped? "Did you think I stayed here?"

"You. . .you went to America?" He backed away from her. She felt his absence like the gust of a Siberian wind.

"Didn't you know? I left a note with Aranoff. I was. . ." No, she could tell by the look on his face, Aranoff hadn't delivered the message that she was pregnant.

Why not?

"Was what?" Mickey's face darkened. "Annulling our marriage?"

Shock left her mouth open, her heart spilling out. "Annulling?"

He lifted his hands as if to push away her words. "Fine. Listen, I understand, I do." He stood up, turned away from her, his head shaking. "I would have done the same, in your position. I really don't blame you."

Only he looked like he'd been gutted, the way he braced his arm against the doorframe as if needing it for support. "It's probably for the best."

She was the one who needed support. "I. . .didn't. . . annul our marriage."

He turned, and her heart wrung out at the way his eyes had filled, his jaw had tightened.

"You should. Because I'm not going back to America with you, Nadia. I'm staying here in Russia and finishing my mission."

If he wasn't the jerk of the year before, he'd win the prize now. One glance at Nadia, and he knew he'd wounded her. Again.

"I should have guessed. Always the hero, aren't you, Mickey?" She swiped at her tears, and suddenly the conversation they'd had nearly two years ago, on a dark night with the rain pinging the metal roof of their tiny apartment, and hurt edging the tones of her fury, returned to him.

"I don't want a national hero. I just want you."

Both the old and new variations of her indictment spun through his thoughts.

He closed his eyes, wishing he had the courage to back away from this one last mission—had the strength to be just Hope Moore's husband, the way he knew in his gut he should be. But he'd spent over ten years of his life becoming the best in the business, and his entire career culminated in this one mission. Russia's nuclear plans could change the face of the Cold War, push it to eruption. More than that, if Russia could track America's ocean movements from the sky, America would have to change the way she conducted the business of war. Or face annihilation.

American peace, the free world counted on his ability

to stay the course. To say no to the woman he loved.

"I'm not trying to be a hero. I'm just doing my job."

"A job I thought included loving me."

He flinched. "I do love you." He opened his eyes, and somehow she managed to construct the same incredulous, disbelieving glare she'd given him that night.

"Yeah. Right." She shook her head. "I thought. . .well, I thought gulag might have changed your mind." She nodded. "Okay, fine. You want to finish your mission. Then what?"

He blinked at her. "I'll. . .I don't know."

He would have done less damage if he'd told her he was going to marry Lena, the agent Nadia thought was his mistress. He still stung from her accusation.

Then again, did he think the rumors Aranoff had hinted at wouldn't reach her?

"Fine," she said, rebounding like a pro. "Tell ya what. I'm going to help you finish this all-important mission, and then we'll duke it out. I want you to come home, Mickey. To the home I made for us in America." She swallowed, and she looked like she might be gathering the ammunition for another chops-ringing smack. But instead, she sighed, a deep gust of sadness. "Maybe your vows didn't mean anything to you, but to me. . .well, I was serious. I'm not annulling our marriage. I want you to come home." Her voice had pinched tight and high. He looked past her, unable to look at the pain in her eyes. "We. . .I need you."

"No. I want you safe. Out of Russia."

"Out of the way, you mean." She crossed her arms over her chest.

He rubbed his fresh-cut hair, feeling strangely lightheaded. "No, safe. They know you're here, Nadia. Some guard told me a couple nights ago, before he—"

"I only got here a couple days ago." She frowned, and it wiped some of the hurt out of her eyes. A band tightened across his chest.

"Were you followed?"

She shook her head, then shrugged. "Why would they let me get this far if they knew I was going to try and help you escape?"

"Why would they allow me to escape?"

Silence stretched taut between them. Only the rhythmic click of the train swaying on its wheels accompanied their contemplations.

"I'm not going to let them get you again, Mickey." Nadia said it so softly, so resolutely, with determination in her sweet eyes, it arrowed under all his defenses and found the soft flesh of his heart. He winced. She was so easy to love. Every part of her. The tough spy who put her neck on the line for him, the vulnerable woman inside who knew just how to unleash all his protective impulses. Just being around her again made him feel alive. Resurrected. Whole.

"If someone is after you, you need someone to watch your back." She pressed her hand to her chest. "That's me, for better or worse. I'm tired of waiting for you. I came back to Russia to get you, and if you don't want me when this mission is over, then, well, I'll go home." Her voice tightened, as if she pushed back her emotions into a hard ball. "But I'm not going to let you do this alone. I didn't spend ten years of my life sneaking around Russia simply to give it all up now. And guess what. I wanna find out who betrayed you even more than you do. But most of all, I want you home. I. . .don't care what you did with Lena."

He saw what it cost her to lay out her heart when

another tear edged over her eyelid and trailed down her cheek. But she stared at him, hard. His little spook, standing her ground.

"I'm going to the Moscow post office," he heard himself say, as if his brain had detached from his heart. He groaned at the spark of hope in her beautiful golden brown eyes. He sat down opposite her and noticed that they'd entered the city. Mustard yellow, Stalin-era apartments edged the tracks. Wilting weeds and other debris piled against chain-link and green wooden fences that outlined their yards.

"What's there?" She leaned forward, her face alight.

"Proof. I sent you. . .postcards of where I'd been." He measured her expression, hoping to see a spark of recognition. He'd do just about anything for an "Oh, yeah, I got those, Mickey!" right about now.

Nothing. Raised eyebrows. Curiosity on her incredible face.

"They might still be there. And if they are, well, then my mission is complete." *In more ways than one.* He smiled, hope pushing against his fears. Yes, if he could get his hands on his postcards, maybe, just maybe, Nadia would see the truth about his patriotism—and his love. That they'd have to carve out his heart before it belonged to anyone but her and the red, white, and blue.

And where would that revelation put her? In a perfect place to get chopped off at the knees, to see him walk out of her life. . .again. Because, he knew as her eyes searched his, that he wasn't about to go back to America and be a desk jockey in the labyrinth of the CIA. What would he do there? Analyze Russian data? Not after cramming every thought, every spark of energy and talent into this double life. Not after living on the cusp of danger and juggling information between superpowers. He had a purpose beyond himself. Just like she did, right?

Only, staring into her beautiful eyes, why did that purpose seem painfully empty?

"So that means if you find these postcards, you'll come back to America with me?" Her voice had dropped to a near whisper.

What waited for them at home that meant so much to her? A dingy, two-bedroom apartment in the suburbs of NYC? He frowned at her, unable to comprehend why a woman who, only two years ago, had begged to accompany him on his fatal mission—*thank You, Lord, she hadn't*—suddenly wanted to head for the States. Had she turned into June Cleaver, hoping for a white picket fence and children? What happened to his Crazy Hope? His rabble-rouser with spunk?

Hadn't they dreamed about living a life of glory? Nadia and Misha, super spies.

In the sweet corners of his memories, he saw them tracing the dance floors of Russia, sneaking through the halls of the Peter and Paul fortress, hiding in a train bathroom. The adventure, the adrenaline—it defined them, pushed their love to places that life in America could never compare.

Yes, she might want him to go home, but maybe, just maybe, he'd convince her to stay.

He traced his finger down her creamy face, touched the barest hint of her smile. "That means my home is with you, baby."

CHAPTER SEVEN

Maria took a long drag on a cigarette and watched Misha and his pretty bride disembark—from opposite ends of the train, of course. The two separated and threaded through the crowd like the covert operators they were. The midmorning sun gilded the train platform, a golden carpet to usher in the prizes. A smile tweaked the agent's lips, knowing the ruse had worked. Misha had returned to Moscow, to his playground of espionage, and maybe back into the lives of his sleepers. And if Maria's plan didn't work, they'd resort to phase two. Misha would spill everything when Nadia's tortured cries reached his ears. Still, maybe they wouldn't have to involve her at all.

Maybe Misha would simply lead them to his ring of agents, those betrayers of the Motherland, lurking among the loyal population.

It would be better if Edward Neumann's daughter wasn't a part of the carnage. The repercussions were too great. Besides, Maria hated to see Nadia's pretty face scarred, even if the woman had been nothing but a thorn in the flesh.

Still, for the sake of communism, sometimes lives had to be sacrificed.

Maria knew that way too well. Lives and souls.

Something Misha should have thought of ten years ago when he dared recruit his agents from the congregation of Moscow University students.

Did he seriously think they could outwit a Russian?

Maria flicked away the cigarette and watched it sizzle in a half-frozen puddle. Glory and honor came to those who waited. Patiently.

Nadia stalked through Red Square, scattering a clump of gray pigeons. Her heart marched twenty feet in front of her, pinned squarely on Mickey's wide shoulders. She'd been on his tail since the train, convinced, finally, that he wasn't trying to ditch her.

Maybe, just maybe, she could believe him.

His words dug themselves farther into her heart. "My home is with you, baby."

She allowed herself a full breath and noticed how cleansing it felt to finally embrace hope.

The fact that he'd actually feared she'd had their marriage annulled. . .well it went past seeding hope and pushed it into full bloom.

Yes, gulag had changed him. Ripped the scales from his eyes to show him where his priorities should lie. Showed him who loved him.

Perhaps, indeed, he hadn't betrayed her. He hadn't betrayed his country, either, right?

Mickey Moore was the man of honor she'd known and loved from the first day she'd been assigned to him. Despite her father's predictions, his evisceration of Mickey's character when she'd arrived home with a child in her womb.

She couldn't wait to prove her father wrong. *It wasn't*

a mistake to marry him, Dad.

Kat, he's coming home. Just wait until Mickey saw their daughter, took in her caramel hair, those beautiful amber brown eyes, her lopsided smile. The image of baby Kat, hands slapping the table as she begged for her next bite of strained peas, pushed a smile up Nadia's face, and she had to fight her expression back into submission. Just the thought of her daughter's baby-fresh scent filled her chest with tender feelings. Her heart ached with missing Ekaterina. Yes, Mickey would fall head over tail in love with their daughter. The fact that he didn't know made her feel somehow devious, but the last thing she wanted to give him right now was more ammunition to send her packing. She had every intention of watching his back until they completed his job and they could get on with the mission of living.

My home is with you, baby. And after the kiss that had left her wrung out and weak, she believed it. Nadia nearly skipped and forced herself to trudge along as if fighting the crisp November wind. A gust picked up a layer of garbage and dirt and tumbled it across the huge parade square, toward Lenin's mausoleum. Two green-uniformed guards started straight ahead, flanking a line that formed between metal barricades to view the remains of the father of communism. A father who still seemed very much alive. Lenin ogled them from huge portraits lining the streets, from statues on the street corners, from pictures in the state's department store. Lenin lived, and every day Russia still trembled under his grip.

Nadia picked up her pace and kept her head down, realizing again how free she'd felt when she'd finally dusted the soil of the USSR off her shoes.

Under her wig, perspiration gathered, but her hair felt greasy, and she had the unhappy sense that she reeked like something that slept under the depot. Mickey's vodka odor had rubbed off on her, perhaps. But the fact that she looked and felt like a hobo wouldn't deter her from gluing herself to Mickey's tail as he beelined to the post office.

Postcards? She had a hard time understanding what sort of proof might be contained in a bunch of flimsy mail, but the guy had a steel look in those green eyes, and she knew in her heart that he wasn't lying.

Mickey paused on the corner of Tverskaya Street and Dzerinksy Prospect, then crossed with the flow. She tagged along on the far edge of the crowd, stopping on the far corner to buy a *peroshke.* She felt so ravenous she could probably eat a reindeer raw, but she nibbled the fried bread slowly. Choking wouldn't be in her best interest at the moment.

The Moscow Central Post Office was located on Tverskaya Street. Nadia strolled in with a clump of babushkas and purchased a *Moscow Times* newspaper. She remembered when the *Times* had been a regular form of communication between her and Aranoff during the days when she played courier and he climbed the KGB ranks, becoming one of America's most important assets.

Out of the corner of her eye, she watched Mickey disappear around to the backside of an endless row of wooden post office boxes. He'd obtained the central key from the desk by giving his box number and key code. She tensed and, out of habit, opened the paper.

Mickey's picture was plastered on the inside front page. A young Mickey, the one she'd met ten years ago with tousled hair and mischief in his eyes. He looked slyly into the camera, which translated into pure dare on the printed page.

Below his picture, she read, *"Smert Shpeonia."*

Death to Spies.

She swallowed, backed herself against the wall, and began to read.

"Michael Moore, convicted of espionage against the USSR, died yesterday during an escape attempt from Gorkilov Prison. Known for over a decade of covert activities while serving as a diplomatic liaison to the American consulate, Mr. Moore showed his loyalties before death by betraying his fellow countrymen. His information and death put an end to the traitorous exploits of more than twenty enemies of the Motherland, spies the Ministry of State Protection will ferret out and punish for their treachery."

"Nadia?" Mickey stood a meter away, staring out the window, reading a copy of *Pravda,* the official Russian propaganda rag.

She closed the paper, tucked it under her arm, feeling sick. "Let's go."

He frowned, but she stalked past him, barely able to breathe.

Dead? Okay, so she knew that much wasn't true. But a traitor? Her chest felt tight. She needed air and gulped it as she fast-walked down *Centralnaya,* weaving in and out of Muscovites huddled against the cold, their wide stony faces lending bulwark to her emotions that wanted to spill out onto the street.

No.

"Nadezhda!" She heard Mickey's voice call her. Tucking her head, she sped up, now blinded by idiotic tears that proved she must have believed the lies. Aranoff had told her Mickey had betrayed them. Why hadn't she listened? Why had she thought the invincible Mickey might be above the vises of the KGB?

Why had she risked her life for a trait—

"Nadia!" He grabbed her arm and muscled her into an alley between two towering apartment buildings. Her heart pounded in her throat, and she looked away, unable to face him.

Had she married a. . .traitor?

"What is it?" Mickey cupped his hand under her chin, raised her face to meet his eyes. They were red-rimmed, either from fatigue or fear. And the way he searched her face—with such concern—it only tangled her confusion into a hard, cold ball.

"What happened in there, Mickey?" She wrenched her chin out of his grasp. "Did. . .they. . .okay, I can understand, I really can. . . ." Her voice shook. She sucked in a breath and fought for composure. "Of course, no one would expect you to hold up. I mean, the fact that you lasted this long should count for something, right?" Yes, sure. He'd lived for over a year because they hadn't been able to torture the truth out of him. Until the end, of course.

"What are you talking about?" He stepped away from her as if she had suddenly become radioactive.

Her heart turned over, unable to bear the thought of how it might have felt—*please, no!*—to betray the people he cared about.

"It's okay, Mickey. They'll understand. After all, it was torture."

He frowned at her. Looked at the paper. Swiped it out of her hands and fumbled with it until he found the article.

She watched his face change, his expression shake, as if all his emotions converged on the edge, threatening to push through. He crumpled the paper, threw it to the ground, and closed his eyes.

"They're lying."

Nadia stared at him. At his clenched jaw. At the way his eyebrow twitched, a sure sign of frustration, and suddenly all she saw was the man she'd loved. The vulnerable Mickey who had once told her that he'd give his life for his country. The Mickey who had tried to protect her over and over, to the point of fury. She'd once claimed to trust him. To see past his layers. To know him.

"You didn't betray them, did you?"

He shook his head, then opened his eyes and gave her a look that made her want to cry. "No."

"It's okay, Mickey." She stepped close, put her arms around him, and buried her face into his jacket. She felt him shudder. Then he put his arms around her and held her.

They hung on as the Moscow traffic hustled by, as the road filled with exhaust, as a cloud drifted over the late morning sun and enshrouded them in shadow.

"We'll prove you didn't do this," Nadia said into the folds of his wool militia jacket.

He shook his head. "No, we won't. Other than the passports Aranoff left, the PO box is empty. For all HQ knows, I'm a traitor."

"I gotta get you home." Any thought of resurrecting the famous Nadia and Misha, heroes of the Cold War, died as he stood in the dank alleyway, holding onto his last shred of hope. The fact Nadia trusted him felt like the only ember in his suddenly frigid future.

"Yes, Mickey. We'll go home. Daddy will understand. He'll fix it—"

"Hardly." Mickey put her away from him, trying to

keep all the emotions he had about her father from showing on his face. "Nadia, your dad. . .well, he was right. I'm just trouble for you." He shook his head. "Edward is not going to fix this. On the contrary, he'll do whatever it takes to get me tried and hung."

She backed away. "That's not true. He might not be happy about our marriage—"

"Happy? Baby, he practically threatened to have me shot and quartered." He put his hands to his head, shaking it as he turned away from her. She gripped his arm.

"Okay, so we both know that you weren't his favorite person. It's no secret that he didn't love me working for the company. But he. . ." She frowned. "Shot *and* quartered?"

He glanced at her. A smile edged up her face. "And you married me anyway?"

"That's not funny, Nadia. You know your dad has the power to. . .well you could be visiting me in Leavenworth for the next two lifetimes."

He stalked farther into the alley. "I can't believe this. What was I thinking?"

He should have guessed the KGB would twist his escape to their advantage. After all, that was what this seashell game was all about. Lies, deceit. Weariness nearly staggered him. He turned back to Nadia, defeated.

She was white. She stared at him, swallowed hard. "I don't know what you were thinking, Mickey. Maybe you're right. Maybe this was a mistake. From the beginning."

What?

He frowned at her, but she turned and started to stalk out of the alley to. . .where? He raced for her, grabbed her arm, whirled her. "Hello? Did I miss something?"

"What were you thinking? As in, *why did you marry*

me?" Her cute chin trembled, and he felt like a dog.

Of course, that wasn't what he meant. His marriage to her was the one sure thing in this chaotic, painful world he'd done right. It had never been a mistake to love her, at least on his end. Loving her had made life. . .full. Complete. Honest. In a world fabricated by deceit, her love, her ability to see beneath the layers centered him. At the end of the day, he shrugged off the mantle of Misha, covert Russian handler, and became Mickey.

No, he'd never regret marrying her. . .if he only thought about his own needs. But now Nadia could never live a normal life. Either he'd have to escape Russia and live life on the lam, always glancing over his shoulder, sorting through allies to his true friends. Or worse, he could go home, face the firing squad, and best-case scenario, spend his life in a three-by-four-foot cell in Kansas.

And there wouldn't be any fluffy snow drifting into his window to lull him into a painless hypothermic death.

He'd be lucky if he ever saw snow again.

Maybe it would have been better just to let the KGB shoot him. Then Nadia wouldn't be pacing in a circle in a dark alley, staring at him as if he'd just plunged a dagger into her heart. And he wouldn't have to face Edward's prophecies and condemnations. He wouldn't have to live under the specter of traitor.

He wouldn't have to surrender the one thing he wanted more than anything in the world.

Nadia.

He took a deep breath, intending to deny her words. *Why did you marry me?* Except maybe. . .

Yes. That was exactly what she should think. That he'd made a horrible mistake.

He breathed through his vise-tight chest, willing himself to do the one right thing for her, for once in his life, and forced the words out. "Yeah, what was I thinking?" He shook his head as if in disbelief. "I should have listened to your father from day one."

"What?"

"You heard me. I should never have married you. Edward is going to have my hide if he catches me. Which he's not. And the first thing to throw him off my trail is your putting your cute fanny on an airplane and heading home."

"What?"

He hated how her voice trembled and had to fight not to take her into his arms, not to tremble himself.

"Nadia, I want you to go home. Forget you met me. Forget you made the biggest mistake ever." He tore his gaze away from her tortured expression, the pain so palpable he wanted to howl. "I repeat. Annul our marriage. I was a fool to think we could resurrect what we'd had."

Tears glazed her eyes, but behind them, he saw the slightest edging of anger. *Yes, that's right, baby, hate me. Dump me now.* He steeled his emotions, hating himself even more than she ever could.

"Well, you might be right about that, Jack. Maybe marrying you was the biggest mistake of my life." Her voice turned low, dangerous and lifted the fine hairs off his neck. "But think of this, Mr. Benedict Arnold. The KGB knows I'm here. You're not going to get me fifty meters near an airport without getting you. . .and me arrested."

He frowned at her. This from the woman who passed herself off as a Russian violinist and actually played in the pit of the Bolshoi to keep her cover? She could do a pirouette under their noses, singing a tune from Three Dog Night, and they'd think she was a Russian pop-star wannabe.

"Fine. I know someone who can get you over the border while I figure out how to disappear." He grabbed her arm. She hit him across the stomach, and pain spiked into his brain as his wounded ribs screamed. He gasped, doubled over, reached out for purchase on the wall before he crumpled.

"Oh, Mickey, I'm sorry."

It took all his training not to melt into her concern. He scraped up a growl. "No problem, Nadia. I know what you think of me." Clinging to the grimy side of a building, he forced himself to straighten. She might have knocked something loose, but he bit back the groan that wanted to surface.

"C'mon." He hobbled toward the street, picking up speed as he went, thankful that he could still fake it with the masters. He heard her behind him.

"Where are we going?"

He paused, already pained at his answer. Good thing she wasn't in front of him because he was pretty sure his expression betrayed the cost of his answer. "Lena Chornova's house." His so-called mistress.

He heard her tiny gasp as they melted into the flow of street traffic. She marched beside him, master of disguises that she was, held her head high, and didn't betray for a second that he might have dealt her a blow right to her heart.

If Edward, Nadia, and the rest of the American espionage network didn't hate him now, they would before the night was over.

CHAPTER EIGHT

Mickey was taking her to Lena's house?

Nadia felt as if she dragged her entrails down the street as she followed in his shadow.

Just exactly how had she gone from having Mickey in her arms, nearly swooning with the hope that they might find some measure of happiness as a family, to life crumpling in her grip?

Ditch him. Now. Ditch. Run. She knew where the safe houses in the city were. She could call her father, and he'd come running. If he wasn't already here.

And then what? *Dad, you were right?* If it were possible, that thought made her feel worse. No, she'd been the brilliant one who bought a plane ticket and practically sprinted back to pain. She would grit it out. Until tomorrow, when she'd happily let Lena smuggle her out of the country. . .and out of Mickey's life. The little sparrow could have the two-timing weasel.

She took a swipe at her already gritty eyes, balled her fists, and held her head up.

The smell of dust, greasy *cheboriki* sandwiches, and motor exhaust twisted her stomach as they descended to the subway. She felt Mickey's eyes on her as she wheedled through the crowd to a place on the end of the platform and made herself as tiny as possible. The subways in

Moscow had been constructed during World War II as air-raid shelters, and deep within the city, the air was cool, not frigid, the smell of age and oil seeping from the rails ten feet below. She edged back from the yellow line.

"Nadezhda."

She heard the voice behind her, glanced up, and stifled a cry of shock at seeing Aranoff at her shoulder. He had his head down, a paper under his arm. "Follow me."

She glanced at Mickey, but he had tucked himself behind one of the ornate sculptures in the station. She had no doubts that he had her in his sights as she moved in Aranoff's direction. The subway car rushed in with a gulp of air, and Nadia followed him into the car. She sat. Aranoff turned to face the front, one hand on the strap.

"They know you're in Moscow."

A thrill of fear chilled her. "Do they know where we are?"

He shrugged. "The package I delivered will no longer work. I'll have to think of a new plan."

She nodded.

"Where will you go?"

She could barely form the name above a swell of pain and shame. "Lena's," she choked.

He looked at her then, one sleek eyebrow up, and in his eyes she saw pity. *No, don't, Aranoff.*

She looked away, biting her lip.

"Ladna. I'll call you."

He moved away into the crowd, but she felt the sting of his question and her answer in his wake. She closed her eyes, recalling his words spoken over two years ago in her tiny, one-room apartment. She still remembered the hum of the refrigerator, the plunk of water out of their leaky faucet. "What will you do?" he asked as he straddled a kitchen chair backward, a mere three days after she'd discovered her pregnancy. She was still warm with the glow.

"I'll wait and tell him when he gets back," she'd answered him. Aranoff had a ragged look that day, whiskers roughening his usually clean-shaven chin, circles under his eyes. She remembered, especially, how he'd taken her hand, smoothed his thumb over hers. "Go home, Nadezhda. Go home."

She frowned, and her heart skipped at his low tones, sounding nearly like a warning. Or a threat.

"Why?" she breathed.

"Because. . .Mickey doesn't want a baby. He'll be. . . angry."

She shook her head. "That's not true." But inside, fear dampened her confidence. "He'll be happy."

"He'll be frustrated. He lives for the company. You know that." He shook his head, his pale blue eyes searching hers, finally filling with pain. "Besides, you aren't the only one who wanted to give him a child."

She'd swallowed, twice, hearing her world, or maybe her heart, cracking around her. "What?"

"Lena also carried his child. A few years ago." Sadness tugged at his expression.

"How do you know?" she'd asked and tried to hide the way she felt like she just might choke.

"She's my cousin. She told me everything, and how Mickey forced her. . .to. . ." He cringed and looked away and Nadia died inside. Mickey and Lena? But Mickey had said that it was all a cover. . .that he'd never once been anything but a gentleman to his sparrow. Ever.

Perhaps Nadia had believed him too easily. Except, she had seen them dancing together, more than once, and hadn't he himself told Nadia that Lena was his most important asset? How important, exactly?

She felt ill, had pushed herself from the table and run to the bathroom.

Aranoff left some time later, closing the door with a soft click. In the end, he'd driven her to the airport and had promised to deliver the letter she'd written. The one where she poured out her hopes and prayers that Mickey would want her. . .and their child.

Still, somehow over the past two years, she'd talked herself into believing that Aranoff had lied. But Mickey hadn't exactly come running, even if he hadn't known about the baby, had he?

In fact, when she'd begged him not to go in the first place, he'd nearly laughed. And now he was bringing her to Lena's house?

Fool! Fool! Fool!

She nearly jumped up and ran after Aranoff. Why, oh why, hadn't she married him when he asked?

She sucked a deep breath and forced her hands together in her lap. She would survive. Somehow she'd go to Lena's, endure her reunion with Mickey, agree to the escape plan, and then she'd shut the door on this heart-wrenching chapter of her life.

And admit to her father that she'd made the worst mistake of her life.

If Lena Chornova felt surprise at seeing him, the woman masked it like a professional. A smile graced her pretty, slim face, and she moved aside and held her door open without a word.

Nadia, however, made a fuss, eyeing Lena like she might bite.

Mickey wondered, suddenly, if Lena might have more to fear from Nadia.

Once the door closed, Lena put a finger to her lips, then stalked to her kitchen and cranked the volume on the state-installed radio hanging on her kitchen wall. The flat filled with the garbled voice of party-sanctioned propaganda. The memory of their own apartment, complete with their designated enclaves for serious communication, rattled through Mickey with, of course, the echo of Nadia's voice in his ear, sometimes intimate, other times furious and controlled. Trying to ignore the dull throb in his chest, he glanced at her as she followed him in and leaned against the wall.

Lena turned, and her pretty face crumbled, those green eyes filled, and she launched herself in his arms, showing more emotion for her handler than she had the entire ten years he'd known her. "Misha, I was afraid. I thought they had. . .that you were." She tightened her arms around his neck. "You're alive."

Out of the corner of his eyes, he saw Nadia drop her bag and cross her arms, indictment screaming from her expression. He winced and put Lena away from him. She'd aged in a year, visible lines of worry in her gaunt face, her blond hair more coarse, her eyes pained. She must have dropped ten pounds at least, something that made her look more scarecrow than sixties chic. "Thanks for taking me in."

A slight smile touched her lips. Then she turned to Nadia. "You came for him."

Nadia nodded, brown eyes cool.

"You're very brave." She glanced at Misha. "And loyal." She turned, smiling, and patted Misha on the lapel. "You don't deserve her, you know."

He nodded but couldn't look at Nadia as she peeled off her leather jacket. He took off his shoes, thankful to be out of them. Next time he mugged a militia officer, he'd find one who had feet *larger* than his. He practically hobbled to Lena's tiny kitchen, suddenly comforted by the smell of pickles, salted cabbage, and old tea. He plopped down on a stool. Lena lit her tiny gas stove and measured out fresh tea into a ceramic pot.

Nadia took up a cautious position against the doorjamb, arms crossed, looking like a thug. A soprano, singing a piece from one of the current operettas, shrilled from the radio.

Mickey kept his voice low. "Lena, I need to get Nadia out of the country."

Lena glanced over her shoulder, another tweak of a smile. "That won't be easy. Your picture is on the television. They'll be looking for you."

"Not me. Nadia. I'm staying here." He refused to grimace as he said it but saw Nadia close her eyes. *I'm sorry.*

Lena turned and leaned her hip on the counter. She held a hot pot in one hand. Wearing a green housedress and a pair of ragged slippers, her blond hair falling out of a loose bun on top of her head, she looked so far removed from the woman who had danced the lead in *Swan Lake* or cajoled her way into the private conversations of party officials. She looked tired. Old.

He felt a twinge of pity at what this job had cost her.

"You're staying?" She shook her head. "Mish, it isn't safe. You need to go home. To your family."

Nadia glanced at her, and Mickey didn't miss a slight scowl.

"Someone took the pictures I had of the RORSAT-Ocean Surveillance Satellite systems. I sent them to my post office box for Nadia to pick up." He avoided looking at her, smarting anew at the fact that she'd ditched town when he'd needed her. "She never got them, but they're gone."

Lena frowned, swallowed, turned back to the pot on the stove, which had begun to pump out steam. "Is it worth your life?"

"Or the lives of those who died in your place?" Nadia snapped.

He stared at her, his chest tight. She didn't think. . .

"What about Wilson and Sukharov? They were caught. Executed." Nadia's voice held an unfamiliar edge.

Lena had her back to them, but she'd stiffened.

"Or didn't you think that your betraying them would mean their death sentence?"

Mickey stared at her. "I didn't betray them. I said nothing about them."

Nadia shook her head. "I need to use the WC. You're making me ill." The tiny flat nearly shook as she traipsed down the hall to the bathroom.

"Did you see Aranoff?" Lena's voice fell as if trying to conceal her words from Nadia. She turned, holding the teapot full of *kepitoke,* the spicy Russian tea concentrate.

"No, I. . .of course not. He doesn't know I'm here."

She set down the pot. "I see." She frowned. "I thought maybe he'd helped—*Ladna,* I'll call him, see what he can arrange."

He covered her hand with his. It was still bony and tough, just like her. She smiled, and this time it touched her eyes. "I missed you, Misha. I was very worried."

"Sorry to interrupt." Nadia stood at the door. Hurt washed through her eyes as she glanced at their clutched hands. "I'm pretty tired. Do you mind if I take a bath, Lena?"

Lena withdrew her hand from Misha's. *"Nyet problema.* I'll get you a towel." She moved past Nadia, and Misha half expected his wife to do a kung fu move and flatten the woman in the doorway. He tensed, prepared to jump between them, aching that he'd concocted this mess.

He should have guessed Nadia would believe the rumors, despite his best attempts to prove to her that she would always be the only woman he loved. A good agent needed a cover. . .and Lena had, on more than one occasion, provided the community at large with ample reason to believe they might be an item.

Still, he felt like a jerk to see Nadia wounded.

He nearly followed her into the bathroom, an explanation on his lips. But he'd deliberately brought her here, yes, to elicit Lena's help, but also to fertilize the forget-me-I'm-trouble seeds he'd dropped in the alleyway.

He'd reiterate his desire for an annulment a few more times, as well. If he didn't choke on the word.

Lena returned, sat down opposite him at the tiny wooden table, and pulled out two saucers. She poured a few teaspoons of *kepitoke* into the bottom of the saucer and handed it to him, pushing the sugar bowl toward him.

He picked up the saucer, chose a sugar cube, dipped it into the brown liquid, and then sucked the juice from the bottom of the cube. Russian adrenaline. Lena mimicked his movements.

"How is General Pashov?" he asked.

She shrugged, hiding as usual how deeply she felt, and hurt, over her longtime love. What he hadn't realized the night he'd wooed Nadia into his arms was that Lena was also falling hard for her contact. She walked a thin line of deceit and love and never felt comfortable on either side. Not seeing her for two years made Misha realize how her double life ate at her.

"Working hard," she answered. Translation: The general hadn't figured out that he had a woman who loved him, willing to devote her life to him. Instead, he still vied for the party's affections. Mickey had to wonder: If the man ever caught on, would they lose one of their most important assets?

"I'm sorry, Lena."

She shrugged her bony shoulders. Her skin looked so pale, nearly sickly under the dingy kitchen bulb. "Sometimes it makes me angry that I love him so much."

"People make terrible sacrifices for love," he said, meaning to comfort. But she stared at him and slowly nodded. The sound of water running came from the bathroom, mixing with the vibrato of a tenor. Same operetta.

"How did she do it?" Lena asked. She picked out another sugar cube, then angled the dish at him.

Mickey reached for a cube. "I'm afraid to ask. Nadia's always been a bit of a mystery to me. I wouldn't be surprised if she pulled it off on her own."

"Crazy Nadezhda, da?"

"Yeah. I guess." He flinched at the old nickname, amazed at how he'd come to depend on it.

"What about Aranoff? Are you sure he didn't help?"

"I think she would have told me. I don't know." The image of his best friend slugging back vodka shots and slapping him on the back as he told him another KGB tale filled him with melancholy. "Is he okay?"

She shrugged. "I think so. I haven't seen him much since your arrest."

"Hiding out?"

"Lying low. They had a sleeper hunt when they found you. Nadia is right—Wilson and Sukharov were arrested and executed. Rumor was you ratted."

He saw the question flicker in her aged green eyes, so much older than her thirty-two years.

"No. I didn't."

She reached up and traced the bruise on his cheek. "Which is why you got this, I'd guess."

"And more." He finished his second cube and reached for a third, feeling the pure energy already invigorating his veins. "I'm okay, but gulag isn't much fun."

She laughed, a real giggle, something that always made him smile. "Misha, I will miss you when you go home."

He frowned, a smile still on his lips. "I'm not kidding, Lena. I'm not going anywhere."

Her smile faded. "Nyet? Misha, what about your family?"

Oh yeah, his family—his parents in Ohio, his sister and brother on either side of the ocean, living the American dream, complete with Chevys, Little League baseball, and ranch-style homes. They really missed the youngest of the Moore clan. He gave a snort. "They'll be fine. I'll write to my mother and tell her I'm okay."

She scowled at him. "I didn't mean your mother. I meant Nadia. Don't you think you should go home?" She curled a hand over his arm, and he noticed she still kept up with her manicure. "Or did something happen to the baby?"

His heart actually stopped. He heard it screeching to a halt in his chest, and when he opened his mouth, only a tiny hiccup of sound emerged. He took a breath, tried again. "Baby?"

Lena licked her lips. She eyed him without a sound. Swallowed. Then she pushed up from the table and walked out of the room.

Nadia sank down into the bathtub, every muscle in her body starting a slow yawn. Fatigue seeped into her pores, and her eyelids gained about three thousand pounds. Steam spiraled up from the surface of the water like a cup of chai. Moscow water always looked a little like beer, and she played an old game. A mineral bath in the springs of Switzerland. An insane giggle surfaced, and she realized some of her synapses had probably shut down, refusing to fire any longer.

After all, here she was in Mickey's mistress's home, having a bath?

She dunked herself under the water.

The sound of the door slamming brought her back to the surface. "What? Get out!"

Lena stood over her, hand on her skinny hips, fury across her face. "You didn't tell him."

Nadia blinked, wiped water from her face, blinked again. She reached for a towel, but Lena slapped her hand away. It echoed like a gunshot in the tiny cement room. "What is wrong with you?" she demanded.

"I'm at a serious disadvantage here, Lena," Nadia snapped, reaching again for the towel.

Lena gave her hand another slap. "Get over it. Would you rather I get Misha and do this in front of him?"

Her mouth dried. Wouldn't that be fun? She was suddenly achingly aware of the stretch marks across her abdomen, her chest. She crossed her arms and drew up her legs in a feeble attempt to scrape up some grace.

"Misha doesn't know, does he?" Lena crossed her arms. "You didn't tell him."

"Tell. Him. What?" As if her relationship with Mickey was *any* of Lena's business. Nadia's brain really had shut down to even be considering an argument. With Lena. While in her birthday suit. She glared at the sparrow.

"You didn't tell him about the baby. You did have his child, right?"

Nadia's eyes widened. She swallowed. "What did you say to him?"

Lena held out her hands in surrender. "I thought he knew. What was I supposed to say? He says he is staying in Russia. I asked him why he wasn't going back to his family. You should see him—" She indicated the closed door, where on the other side Nadia's baffled husband probably stood, one ear slicked against the door. A shiver ran up Nadia's spine. "He looks like I hit him with a stick."

"No, your KGB did that," Nadia snarled, unable to stop herself.

Lena glared at her. Nadia lifted her jaw, sucked a calming breath. "Listen, for your information, I told him about the baby, and he wasn't interested, thank you very much. You, of all people, should know that."

Oops. She didn't mean for those words to spill out, but they did. Suddenly, Nadia couldn't decide whether to feel justified or just horribly guilty. Who knew but Lena might still be grieving?

Nadia had a sudden, sisterly-type kinship urge to go

and finish the job on Mickey with another big stick.

But Lena just frowned at her. A real, brow-furrowed, confused frown that suddenly had Nadia turning bone cold. "What are you talking about?"

Nadia grimaced, pursed her lips, looked away. "You, ah, were never. . ." Swallow. "Pregnant? With Mickey's. . ."

Lena gave an incredulous huff. "Me? Are you kidding?"

Did Nadia look like she might be kidding? These eight different tones of red certainly didn't have to do with the formerly hot, now quickly cooling, water. "Aranoff told me. . ."

"What?" Lena scowled, and Nadia fought a gathering of acid in the back of her throat.

"Nothing. I'm sorry."

"What did he tell you?" Lena kneeled beside the tub, her voice now softening. Concern edged those green eyes, looking temptingly like friendship.

Nadia looked away at the gathering of hard-water stains around the high-water drain on the tub. "He told me that Mickey made you. . . Well, he didn't really say it, but I got the gist of the conversation. He told me Mickey would never want to be a father. That he loved his job too much."

Lena braced herself on the tub. "And you believed him." She shook her head, as in, *Oh, stupid American*.

It worked. Nadia felt like a worm. "Yes. I. . . Well, you and Mickey were always so. . .friendly."

Lena smiled. *"Maya Americanaya Padruga,* Mickey's heart always belonged to you. From the first moment he met you, he had no other love."

Nadia bit her lower lip, willing back the idiotic rush of tears. She must be very, very tired.

Or a gigantic, world-class fool. She sunk into the

water, letting it cover her chin. Lena reached over and tossed her the towel. "I'm going out to arrange for your escape. Perhaps you can convince your husband to join you."

Nadia closed her eyes and wept as Lena shut the door behind her.

CHAPTER NINE

A baby?

Mickey stalked the length of Lena's family room/sleeping area, all four meters, past the brown and gold area rug, the worn coffee table, along the green-patterned sofa, the brown armchair, and back to the paint-peeling window.

He stood at the sill, watching Lena skirt a group of kids still dressed in school clothes, playing kickball in the weedy yard. She scooted across the street, then disappeared between two buildings on her way to arrange for Nadia's passage out of Russia. Gloomy shadows chased her exit as twilight combined with lumpy cumulus and hovered like doom over the city.

A baby?

So much for an annulment.

He scrubbed his hands over his weary face, not even feeling the bruises. No, his pain radiated from the center of his chest.

The water had stopped running in the bathroom, leaving only the crackle of the radio churning out the Moscow symphony to compete with his drilling pulse for audience. The smell of Lena's perfume, something European, lingered in her narrow, orange floral wall-papered hallway. He had no doubt Pashov's fingerprints imprinted the bottle of fragrance.

Mickey had a child. He tried to get a fix on the emotions boiling in his chest, to narrow down the definition to one. Joy. Fear. Anger. Regret.

A child. His child? Of course. Nadia would never, ever betray him. No wonder she'd begged him to stay in Russia. . .and to come home with her.

My home is with you. He'd said those words, and they took root in his heart. Now more than ever, his home was with Nadia and with his child.

Except, did he forget he was a fugitive? With "Traitor" stamped on his back? And an uncompleted mission?

Never mind the fact that Edward Neumann now had a real, flesh-and-blood reason to want to skin Mickey alive.

All he'd wanted to do was to be a hero. A man of honor, a patriot. He'd wanted to do his job well and come home to the woman he loved.

Or had he? What if the woman he loved lived in Mundane, America? What if he had to surrender the part of him that lived and breathed for a higher purpose?

Had he done anything good? Eternal? Anything other than threaten the life of the woman he loved. . .who was now the mother of his child?

He sat on the sofa, rested his head on his hands.

"Mickey, are you all right?"

He looked up, and his heart jumped to life when he saw Nadia standing in the doorway, her wet hair slicked back, a thin drip of water sliding down her cheek. She wore a pair of Lena's blue nylon sweatpants and a black tee shirt that plastered to her wet body. He felt pretty sure she'd never looked more beautiful.

He groaned. No, no, no, this was *not* going to work.

He could not let himself be the guy who risked his wife's life. The mother of his child's life! He shook his head, closed his eyes, clenched them tight, held his head, and moaned.

"Are you okay?" She moved toward him, and he pounced to his feet, backing away from her. He blew out a breath, aware anew at how fragile, how delicious she looked, all big eyes and wounded expression. And she smelled good. Too good. Like fresh soap and flowers. Sweet and delicate. It dried his mouth, and he broke out in a cool sweat.

Lord, help. I need wisdom here. Help. He suddenly felt like he had the first time he'd met her, dying to hold her, afraid that the minute he touched her, his heart might explode into a thousand tiny fragments. *Danger!* He backed into a corner as his love for his wife grabbed him by the chest and shook him. He'd been so invested in the mission, he hadn't once stopped to consider that he might have been a fool. Reality hit him like a blow in the solar plexus.

He couldn't be a patriot *and* a dad. He'd have to choose.

Please, no. "Nadia, I'm sorry." He gasped, felt his chest tighten. "I am so very, very sorry. I didn't know. I just didn't and if I had, well, I don't know—"

She advanced, guilt all over her pretty face driving his own agony deeper. "Mickey. Lena told me you didn't know about the baby. It's okay."

He put out his hand, held up one finger to stop her. "No, it's not okay. I can't believe you had a baby without me! Where was I?" The thought crippled him, and he braced a hand on the wall behind him. He wanted to hit something hard, to pummel his frustration into something heavy and large. He took a breath, stalked past her, and stood at the window, frustration turning his breath ragged. "What's the child's name?"

"Ekaterina."

A daughter. A little girl, a miniature Nadia. He closed his eyes and put a hand to his chest. "How old is she?"

"A little over a year. She has brown eyes and beautiful light brown hair."

Nadia moved closer; he felt her touch the small of his back. "She has your smile. Crooked and defiantly mischievous."

He couldn't help the groan and hardly realized it when he turned and pulled Nadia into his arms, burying his head in her wet hair. She smelled fresh and young and innocent, and he missed her so much every cell in his body burned.

She lifted her face and met his gaze with those beautiful golden eyes. He'd expected to see anger, hurt, perhaps even disappointment. Instead, at her very core, he saw forgiveness. She smiled, and it completely crushed him.

"Oh Nadia, I'm so, so sorry. I'm sorry I didn't listen to you. I'm sorry I didn't stay home for you, for the baby. Please—"

She hooked her hands behind his neck, drew his head down, and kissed him. Eagerly, full of passion and life and intensity that was pure Nadia. He wrapped his arms about her body, realizing for the first time why she'd looked different. She even felt different in his arms, her body felt fuller, and a new admiration for her courage, her strength, swept through him. He loved this woman with his every breath, every beat of his heart. He drank in her kiss and kissed her back, not realizing how badly he'd missed her until she pulled away, and he was left breathless, on the raw edge of desire.

She smiled and urged him over to the sofa. "Mickey,

there are many things I've regretted over the past two years. Having your child is not one of them."

She sat, lifted her face, and smiled at him. As he knelt before her, he knew that saying good-bye to her again would rip out his heart.

It wouldn't matter if the KGB found him. He'd already be dead.

He gathered her in his arms, ready to kiss her until he forgot about his mistakes, his dark tomorrows, when the telephone rang.

Nadia jumped, then gave a little giggle. It found all the soft soil in his heart, the places where his love for her had already grown into a tangled forest.

"I'm not used to. . .kissing."

He smiled at that. "Good."

She reached for the telephone. He put his hand over hers. It rang again.

"What are you doing?" he asked, wondering if she'd forgotten they were fugitives.

The look on her face froze time. She paled, closed her mouth, and suddenly everything sweet between them died with a gut-wrenching moan. "It might be Aranoff. I'm expecting his call."

"Aranoff helped you plan this?"

She cringed, felt herself go numb as she withdrew her reach from the telephone. It shrilled again as she turned and nodded. "He didn't want me to tell you."

Mickey backed away from her, stood, and stalked across the room. She recognized his controlled, Mickey-style fury in his low tone, the slight tremble in his shoulders.

"You know how important Aranoff is. If he is compromised, it could destroy a decade of work. He'll be executed on the spot." He pressed his hand on his forehead. "What were you thinking?"

She stared at him. "I was thinking about you, Mickey. About our daughter never having a daddy."

But he wasn't listening. He began to pace the room again, this time muttering under his breath. She rose, went over to touch him. He bristled. "You shouldn't have come here." The words, so softly spoken, decimated her without mercy. He stepped away from her. "You should have let them kill me."

Tears burned her eyes, and she swiped them back. "Why? Because your life isn't as valuable as Aranoff's? Because you're not worth saving?"

"Yes!" He rounded on her. "Yes. Don't you see, Nadia? I'm a failure. I'm an embarrassment. At best, the CIA will cut out my tongue and expunge my name from their records. You'd have been better off as a widow." His eyes had turned red, and little lines betrayed both his anger and his fatigue. He clenched his jaw as if trying to hold back his own tears, and he stalked across the room toward the ringing telephone. "I wish you'd never come back."

I wish you'd never come back. Her eyes felt thick as she forced them open and found that the hues of night had stormed into the room while she'd cried herself into an exhausted slumber on the sofa. The apartment felt strangely quiet. The radio had been turned down, or perhaps they'd simply given the entire country a reprieve. She couldn't hear Mickey's voice on the telephone in the other room, talking with Aranoff, as she had when she first lay down, wrung out and utterly crushed by Mickey's cruel words.

I wish you'd never come back.

At this point, she did, too.

She pushed herself off the orange crocheted pillow, pretty sure she'd etched the pattern into her cheek. The overhead moon gave wan light to the room, and she fumbled on the end table before she clicked on the metallic lamp. Light bathed the carpet, turning it muddy brown.

"Mickey?"

Nothing but the sound of her swelling heartbeat. Panic slid up her throat. He hadn't ditched her, had he?

She rose, padded into the hall, saw that his shoes were gone, and flicked on the light to the kitchen.

A note on the table. With her name.

Her hand shook as she picked up the tablet paper, read the scrawled pencil message on gray, red-lined paper.

"Nadia. I'm sorry I hurt you. Go home and forget about me. For the sake of our daughter. Michael.

Not Mickey. Michael Moore, career spy.

She crumpled into a ball and slid down the wall, leaned her forehead into her knees, and fought tears.

Perfect, just perfect. She'd managed to bring about her worst fears. Mickey wasn't coming home.

Which meant Ekaterina would grow up without a father. Because there was no way Nadia was going to hand out her heart again. For anyone.

She was about as successful at getting the men in her life to love her as the peace protesters were at stopping the Vietnam War.

Her father spent his entire life running around Russia, desperate, it felt, to bring about the end of communism. Or were his goals more personal? It seemed to her that even when he was home on the farm, helping her with her math homework or teaching her to drive, his mind was divided. Always wrapped around something. . .or someone else. She'd long ago accepted that her pleading, her good behavior, even the years lived in teenage rebellion weren't going to make him turn his entire, 100 percent-plus attention on her.

Obviously, she had no better effect on her husband.

So, what was it about her that made men run?

She'd believed that by emulating her father, by proving to Mickey that she could not only keep up but best them both, she'd earn their respect. Their devotion. Their love.

Yeah, right.

She crumpled the note and threw it against the wall.

Maybe it was time to go home. Back to Ekaterina. Back to the one person who loved her with abandon.

"Yea, I have loved thee with an everlasting love."

She stilled, hearing the soft voice inside, trying to wrap her brain around the words. Grandma's voice. Roughened with age, softened by love. Reading. . .her Bible? In Nadia's mind's eye, she tracked back to the times she'd sat on the rag rug, playing with her dolls, or more often, arranging for her dolls to be captured—and rescued—by Bart, her ratty teddy bear.

"Can a woman forget her sucking child, that she should not have compassion on the son of her womb? Yea, they may forget, yet will I not forget thee."

She held her breath, letting the words sink deep, feeling them tingle in her soul. She'd only just stopped nursing Ekaterina. She easily recalled the way her body reacted when her child cried. Even if she wanted to push Ekaterina out of her mind, wanted to walk away from her pleas, her body wouldn't let her. It reacted to her child on its own, reaching out to love her. To nourish her.

God loved her like a nursing mother—His natural bent to protect, to nurture?

The God of the universe loved *her*. . .like she loved Ekaterina?

Nadia pressed her fingertips into her eyes to stem her tears. What was she doing in Russia, trying to reel in her husband's, even her father's love when she already had the unwavering love of her heavenly Father?

She *had* been foolish. Made the worst mistake possible. She'd thirsted after love and tried to quench it with the fickle attention of her father, her husband, when instead she should have slaked it on the never-ending nourishment of the Lord. No wonder she felt bereft of faith and wisdom. She'd searched for it in the wrong place.

Her throat thickened. "I've been such a fool, Lord." She wiped her palms down her face, lifted her gaze to the ceiling past the crack that ran from the dusty orange fixture and beyond, to where her Father dwelled. She closed her eyes, feeling peace wash through her like a gentle hand running down her back. "Please forgive me for trying to let my father and Mickey take Your place. Your Word says that You alone can satisfy my longing. You alone prefer me. You alone will never leave me or forget me."

She breathed in deeply, felt the knots in her chest loosen, her shoulders slack. "Help me to believe that, to put my faith in You. To see Your love in my life." Sitting in the illuminated kitchen with garbled Russian punctuating the hum of the refrigerator, she felt a quiet strength well in the center of her. "Lo, I am with you always, even unto the end of the world."

She nodded. Mickey had to walk his own path. Alone. She couldn't force him to be the husband for whom she longed. She had to turn her eyes to the only one who could save her. The only one who would return home with her. Forever.

She rose, walked to the sink, washed her face. Maybe it was best if she left in the morning or whenever Lena had arranged. And if she did, she wouldn't look back.

She was toweling off her face when she heard the door click. She slapped off the light, leaned back into the shadow, her gaze on the glass in the kitchen door reflecting a view of the apartment entrance.

Her heartbeat throbbed in her throat as the door opened.

"Hello?"

Lena.

Nadia released her breath. "In here." She turned on the kitchen light and came into view.

Lena closed the door behind her. The woman looked fatigued, gray circles under her eyes. She unwound her silk scarf from her head, removed her jacket, and tucked the scarf into the arm before hanging it in the wardrobe. Bracing one hand on the wall, she worked off her high boots. "I'm sorry I took so long. It'll take a day or two, but I think I can get you out through our Finnish connections. Until then, I want you and Misha to go to the safe house."

"Mickey's not here."

Lena looked up, panic streaking her expression. "Where did he go?"

Nadia shook her head. "I don't know. We. . .had a fight."

Lena finished pulling off her boots, set them side-by-side on a tiny rug, then turned and gave Nadia a look of disappointment. "You didn't believe me."

"No, that's not it. In fact. . ." She swallowed hard against the memory of how Mickey had trembled at her touch. In that moment, she had been sure he would return her love, Mickey-style. But as soon as she betrayed her liaison with Aranoff, she could nearly hear the locks turning in his emotional bulwark, and he'd flicked her away as if she had a case of head lice. "He doesn't want me. He left a note and ordered me to go home."

Lena raised one eyebrow, then shook her head. "He wants you. More than he wants to admit, perhaps, but he wants you." She reached down to retrieve the bag she'd dropped by the door. "I understand what it means to love a man who doesn't want me, and I'm telling you, every time you walk into a room, Misha lights up. He practically wears his love for you on the outside of his body." She shook her head, rifled around in her black satchel, and pulled out a package. "I stopped by my cache to retrieve this." She held it out to Nadia.

Nadia took the bundle, wrapped in brown paper.

"Open it." Lena dropped her bag, swept past Nadia to the kitchen. "If those don't give you answers, nothing will."

Nadia worked the paper open and nearly went weak when she discovered inside a stack of postcards.

Postcards from Mickey.

"You had these?" Fury simmered in her stomach, and she turned, stalked toward the kitchen. "Mickey needs these."

"You need those." Lena turned the dial of the state radio, filling the kitchen with the sounds of a pianist playing Rachmaninoff. She gave Nadia a pointed, "keep your voice down" look and stalked over to the refrigerator, where she pulled out a bowl of cold potatoes and a jar of pickles. She set them on the table. "I don't know what significance those letters have to Misha, but I'd suggest you read them."

"You picked them up from the post office box?"

"No." Lena opened the pickle jar, fished out a dill. "Aranoff had them. I found them in his apartment a few months ago."

Nadia sat down on the stool, turning over the postcards in her hand, staring at Mickey's scrawled writing. *"Dear Nadia. Every day I awaken, thinking of you. . . ."* She frowned. "Why did Aranoff have them?"

Lena crunched the pickle as she pulled out silverware and set it on the table. "I don't know."

A chill slid through Nadia as she stared at Lena. The bright lights turned her skin waxy, her cheekbones sallow. Even in her green wool sweater, which turned her eyes to a rich jade, the woman looked tired. Up closer, without the dim lights of the nightclub, she saw crow's-feet, the etchings of stress on Lena's otherwise pretty face.

"Did you know who turned on Mickey?" Nadia asked, examining the postcards. Pictures of Almaty, Kazakhstan. "Someone gave the KGB proof of his activities."

Lena pursed her lips, looked down, turned away, and walked to the window. "I've long suspected that my cousin might not be as faithful as he purports."

Nadia froze, her mind tumbling through time. No. Aranoff had always been on their side. Hadn't he been the one who cabled her about Mickey's arrest? Risking his life with outside communication to America? Hadn't he been the one who had hidden them countless times when the KGB raided the flats of other agents, turning up information that sent them home. . .or worse? Hadn't Aranoff watched Mickey's back, slipping him information time and again that kept the Cold War in balance? Neither side winning. . .

She looked at Lena, who turned and met her gaze

with a brows-up look. Lena nodded slowly. A double. An operative who worked both sides?

Then why had he helped Mickey escape? She thought of the thugs who'd been guarding their exit from the train in Kisligorsk, and her chest thickened.

"But he said he was our friend. Mickey's friend." She set the package down on the table, rubbed her fingers across it. "He once told me he loved me."

"I'm afraid he still does, *maya padryga.*" Lena wore a sad expression. "One makes terrible sacrifices for love."

As in turning over his best friend? Had Aranoff exchanged Mickey's life for hers? She closed her eyes. No. "He arranged for our escape. He was the one who gave us tickets out of the country. He met me in the subway and warned me that the KGB was out looking for us." She shook her head. "He even called Mickey with the new plans. I heard Mickey agree to meet him."

"Misha agreed to meet him?"

Nadia's gut tightened. She nodded.

Lena glanced out the window, her expression tight. "You've gotta stop him."

"He's not going to believe me." Nadia glanced at the crumpled note, Mickey's orders to return home. "He'll be furious I disobeyed him."

"Yeah, he will." Lena turned back, but her eyes held a spark of mischief. "Do you love him enough to make him angry?"

He wants you. More than he wants to admit, perhaps, but he wants you. Nadia smiled. "I always have."

CHAPTER TEN

Mickey pushed open the metal door and crept into the tomblike darkness of the metal fabrication factory. Why did Aranoff pick this place to meet? Regrets dug into Mickey's chest like the tiny shards of metallic fibers that littered the dirt floor. No moonlight dinged off the hulking machinery through the high grimy windows, shrouded as they were by a tenacious drizzle. He closed the door behind him and repressed a shiver that started in his cramped, frozen, wet toes and rattled through his body.

The odor of gasoline and burned welds rose from the oily dirt floor, curled around him, and into his nose. He shoved his hands into the pockets of his damp wool jacket and hunched his shoulders, sneaking behind a lathe and crouching in the darkness, eyes on the far door. He could trace the floor plan of the factory floor, knew the path in his sleep, and even now, he felt as if he might be in some sort of nightmare.

Nadia had involved Aranoff. He wanted to howl. His best friend had nearly waved a yellow flag in front of the proverbial wolf, and it would only be a matter of time, and blood, before the KGB sniffed out the truth. Aranoff wouldn't even have the courtesy last meal.

He'd be shot on sight.

Mickey would spend part of this meeting convincing

Aranoff to run with them. To hide out and wait for his cohorts on the other side of the ocean to reel him into safety.

Rats scurried above on the wooden rafters, kicking down debris and dust. Behind their movement, the wind hissed as rain lashed the metal roof. Lightning cracked and illuminated the hooks dangling from the chainlink assembly line. Mickey drew in a breath and coughed. *Aranoff, hurry up.*

He blew on his fingertips, amazed that he could even feel cold after spending months as a side of frozen beef. But everything had changed in the past twenty-four hours. Life had not only become about three billion degrees warmer, but like any part of his body warming after the big chill, he ached from the inside out.

He wondered how Nadia might react to his note. Closing his eyes, he imagined her beautiful golden brown eyes and the spark that lit them dying as she read his words. He knew he'd hurt her, torn a gash right through the soft tissue of her soul when he'd pushed her away. There she was, his wife, offering him forgiveness, hope, a future, and love, and he'd walked right out of her arms. He felt like a skunk.

But even worse would be encouraging her, giving into his impulses and letting her chase him into danger. Better to break her heart than to cost her her life. Every second she spent with him, her safety eroded. And his child's. If only his desires hadn't nearly risen up and grabbed hold of his common sense.

He should be glad Aranoff called. Thankful that Nadia had turned to Mickey's best friend in a time of need.

Yes. Of course. *Nadia had turned to Aranoff.* And his friend had been faithful. Mickey felt slightly ill as his thoughts loosed and ran rampant through his brain. *Nadia and Aranoff.*

Not only would Mickey talk Aranoff into leaving Russia but also into taking with him Mickey's wife. With Mickey's blessing.

Aranoff could fill the role Mickey should have. And wouldn't Aranoff like that? Mickey knew his best friend loved his wife. Aranoff was a poor judge of a spy if he thought that Mickey hadn't noticed the way Aranoff held Nadia when they danced or looked at her as if she might be the most beautiful woman he'd ever seen, tracking her movements across the room.

Yeah, he'd seen Aranoff's desire in his eyes. And until now, it had bothered him. But maybe, just maybe, he could use it to give Nadia the one thing she needed. A father for their daughter. The man he couldn't be.

His chest tightened against the thought, and regret welled in the back of his throat. He pushed through it to a place of peace. Yes, Aranoff would take Nadia home, protect her, be the husband she needed.

He felt hollowed out as he leaned against the wall. Grime embedded his pores, and he listened for movement. Nothing but the rattle of the wind against the loose panes.

A draft clawed at him, and he shivered, not sure if it might be from the future or perhaps the memories, specifically that of Nadia climbing one of the far ladders, dressed in head-to-toe black that only emphasized all her delicious curves.

Curves that he shouldn't be thinking about right now.

That night came back to him with a whoosh, and he remembered well Aranoff's laughter as he lifted his glass to Sasha Borisonovich, well-known party thug and undercover enforcer for the KGB. . .aka assassin. Creeping along the rafters overhead, Nadia planted bugs, hoping to head off the apprehension of any more of their agents. Since the night in Pashov's office, sleepers around Moscow and Leningrad had been disappearing—and showing up again in the Volga River. Someone wanted them dead, and Aranoff thought Sasha just might have the answers.

Mickey had barely been able to breathe as he watched Nadia slink along like a cat. She had courage and ability that turned him numb with worry.

Worry that had built to inferno proportions. After the wardrobe incident, the two days of hiding, of stolen moments in conversation and kisses, she'd handed over her heart. He took it, too, almost greedily. But in exchange, he had been seized by a new and unfamiliar paranoia that she'd be captured.

As he watched his little cat burglar dangle from heights that made him weak, he knew he had to marry her. Regardless of what Edward promised—things that included painful threats—Mickey loved Nadia.

And he'd spend the rest of his life keeping her alive.

As Nadia scrambled through the rafters, Aranoff had out-poured Sasha, toasting until the thug pillowed his angular face into his plate of smoked herring. Aranoff tiptoed out and stood beside Mickey, watching their little spook. Finally, he said, "If you don't catch her, I will."

Regrets clawed at his soul. Mickey should have stepped aside then.

I'm sorry, Nadia.

A door slammed open, caught by a gust of wind. It banged against the wall and ratcheted up his pulse. Mickey huddled in the shadows, feeling very much like a prisoner staring at no-man's-land. Where was Aranoff?

His stomach roared, and he put a hand over it. Groovy. The KGB wouldn't have to see him; they could just follow his empty gut. With some luck, they'd feed him before they put a bullet into the back of his head.

Nyet.

What he wouldn't give for a turkey dinner. Complete with stuffing, mashed potatoes, gravy. His mother's fresh rolls. Molly Moore would like Nadia. They had a similar spirit: His mother knew what it meant to love a man with a dangerous job—namely that of mortar specialist in the European theater. Mickey had feasted on his father's wartime stories, had probably joined the company because of his whetted appetite for adventure and danger.

And the fact that he felt God had actually called him to this. . .this service made it more than just a career. It made it a mission.

He'd never considered he might have to surrender it to the altar of family, even when he married Nadia.

There he went again, thinking like a man who might have a future. A family. Not a man on the run.

And to think he'd dreamed of being a hero just like dear old dad.

I don't want a national hero. I just want you.

He clenched his jaw, dug his fists into his jeans pocket.

"Mickey?"

He jumped and nearly went through his flimsy wool jacket. "Nadia?" Panic grabbed him by the throat. "What are you doing here?"

She moved toward him, a shadow against the darkness. He reached out, and she caught his arm. Her voice turned very soft. "You're in danger."

"Shh. Like that's big news. Get out of here." He grabbed her lapel to keep her in his range of control. Her breath on his chin felt hot, urgent. It raised a flicker of unwanted feelings. Things that had to do with hope and wanting to run with her to a place that they might not have to look over their shoulders.

"*Nyet.* Aranoff knows you're here."

"Of course. He set this up."

"He set *you* up."

Her words took a hiccup beat to sink in. "Repeat, please."

"He. Set. You. Up."

He found his head shaking even before the words came out. "*Nyet.* I don't believe it." He didn't mean to, but his fist tightened in her jacket, pulling her closer. Her lips grazed his cheek, lighting him nearly afire.

This was not the time to think about her lips. Not.

"Nadia. Leave. Now. I want you to go back to Lena's house and wait for Aranoff. I'm going to talk him into defecting. I want you to go home—"

"In your dreams, Jack." She might be hidden in the swaddling of night, but he could see her face in his mind, lit up with fury, sparks in her golden eyes, the set of her jaw, and perhaps her fists clenched take-no-prisoners style. He braced himself.

"You listen to me. I might not have made all the right decisions here, but I promised our little girl that I was going to get you out of Russia, and, Bub, I'm bringing you home." He felt her hand grab his jacket. Her breath streamed into his ear. "I'm not taking any chances, even with Aranoff. Lena thinks he might be a double."

She clamped a hand over his short burst of disbelief.

"Please, just trust me."

He closed his eyes. Trust her. She had gotten him this far. "What do you want?"

"Lena arranged for our escape, but we need to get to our safe house in Pskov first."

He started to shake his head, frustration welling in his chest. Why did she always have to disobey his orders? She was like one of those new neurosurgeons, practicing open brain surgery on her patients—"Does this hurt, Mickey? What about this?"—until, slice and dice, he was unable to talk.

"I don't kn—"

One hand around his neck, she pulled him close and silenced him with a kiss, the kind she'd given him the night he'd asked her to marry him as they walked home from the Bolshoi Theater. The moon had parted the Volga in one golden stripe, and he knew, as he gave away his heart, he would never be whole again. Now, like then, he held her face in his hands and kissed her back, forgetting his resolve, forgetting the mess with Aranoff.

Forgetting that he was the worst possible man for her.

He groaned, fighting the rush of emotions in his chest. She tasted of hope, of sweetness, of rich tomorrows. Nadia was pure adventure, a touch of danger, the woman who loved him. And now the mother of his child.

It brought tears to his eyes, and he fought to blink them away when she backed up, her breath roughened.

The woman always turned his brain into knots. "Nadia." His voice emerged gruffer than he'd intended. "Please, don't do this."

"I'm just trying to save your life," she bit back, obviously hurt. "Again." He gritted his teeth. The last thing he wanted to do was hurt her.

"I don't need you."

Ouch, had he really said that? *Liar, Liar!* He swallowed, licked his lips, which still throbbed from her touch. And it was just his rotten luck that she still smelled so good, pure heaven despite the filth around them.

"I'm meeting Aranoff and sending you home," he ground out.

"Not if he finds you first. Please, trust me, Mickey!"

He opened his mouth, confusion playing with his reply.

A lone flashlight beam striped the walls. Steps, then a voice. "Misha? *Eta Ya,* Aranoff."

"Get down!" Nadia launched herself onto Mickey, her hand clamped over his mouth. His arms tightened around her, strong and solid, despite the year he'd spent suffering. She found his ear, hissed into it. "Just trust me. Please."

He stiffened, but unbelievably, Mr. Do-It-My-Way clamped his mouth shut and simply breathed. In. Out.

"Mish?"

Aranoff's voice, dark, thick, strong made her want to cry. Aranoff, with his pale blue eyes that could see her wounds when no one else could. Aranoff, who alone knew her secrets, her fears. Aranoff, who had helped her return home. . .

And failed to give Mickey her message. Aranoff had kept them apart—deliberately? Maybe. Perhaps out of love. Or. . .jealousy?

Or maybe he was using her. Using Mickey.

The thought thickened her throat, and she couldn't have spoken if she wanted to. *Oh, Lord. Remember Your pledge not to forget me?*

"Misha?"

Thankfully, Mickey had chosen a hiding place near the paint shop, a tiny room with a ventilation system. She yanked on his jacket, willing him to follow her. *Please, don't argue with me!*

As if reading her thoughts, Mickey rose, followed her, crawling through the blackness, down the hall, to the paint room. Aranoff's voice echoed as he called Misha's name.

Nadia scuttled toward the room, feeling dirt and metal shavings and grime dig into her hands, her knees. First thing she'd treat herself to when she returned home—after kissing her daughter—would be a two-hour bath and a good scrubbing with Grandma's homemade lavender soap.

No light seeped into the windowless paint shop, but Nadia traced the room from memory. She stood, grabbed Mickey's jacket, and discovered that he was already on his feet. He nearly took out her chin.

"Air vent," she whispered.

"Why?"

She closed her eyes. Her heartbeat had notched up to high, and a nostalgic rush of adrenaline sluiced through her veins—a rush that made her feel buoyant and nearly invincible. "Because I said so. Because you trained me to know these things. Because I love you."

Silence. She could nearly hear his heart beating as he weighed her words.

Then, miraculously, "Okay. I'll lift you up."

The ventilation system ran into the wall, covered with a grate held on by screws. Mickey grabbed her and hoisted her up onto his shoulders. Nadia pulled out the knife still lodged in her boot and had the screws loosened in less than a minute. She passed the grate down to Mickey. He set it on the ground, then gave her a shove.

"Misha?" The voice sounded closer. Footsteps in the hallway.

"Hurry!" She climbed into the tunnel, turned around, reached down to help him. Her foot accidentally kicked the side and thunder rumbled through the building.

"Shh," he said as he grabbed her hand. He scrabbled up the wall and inside the ventilation duct. "And ditch the shoes."

She scooted down, pulled off her boots.

"Get your fanny moving," Mickey snapped.

She could tell by his tone that he wore a smile. *Oh, yes, Mickey, do you remember the days? The adrenaline surge? The romance?*

She turned and half-slid, half-crawled down the tunnel, wincing when her knee banged too hard, sending a thud against the tubing. But she spied a dent of light at the far end, and if Aranoff heard them, he'd have to cross around the entire block-long building to nab them at the other side.

They crawled to the end, and Nadia peered out through the grate to the ground below—a good twenty feet below.

"Ouch," Mickey said over her shoulder. "You first."

"Thanks," she snapped but laced her boots back on and gave the grate a vicious kick. It groaned but didn't budge.

"Gimmee your knife." Mickey squeezed beside her. She slapped the handle into his palm, and he used the blade like a pry bar. Cement and rust chipped off, and, a moment later, the grate hit the dirt outside with a soft thud.

"Ladies first." Outlined by the dent of night, she could trace the barest hint of a smile. That sweet, scallywag Mickey smile. It did devastating things to her heart, especially at times like these.

"Hold onto me." She backed out of the tunnel, reaching for his hand.

"I thought you'd never ask."

"Funny. Very funny. Just don't let me fall."

He stayed silent, and her heart twisted. Yeah, he was about to let her fall, and hard, the moment he refused to leave Russia.

He didn't contradict her as he lowered her down. She dropped over ten feet, backpedaled, and landed on her feet, her back against the cement wall of the next building.

He followed, and she caught his arm before he went down.

"C'mon!" She angled out toward the end of the alley. He ran one step behind her, his breath coming in heavy gasps. She rounded the corner, gasped, and ducked behind the colossal stone steps of a state-run grocery store. She grabbed Mickey's coat sleeve, and his momentum nearly ripped her arm off as she dragged him into the shadows behind her.

"What?" He leaned over and gripped his knees, breathing hard.

She peeked out for another look, and her heart fell like a rock to her ankles. "Sedans. Black Marias to be exact."

Mickey groaned and she felt the despair in his voice. "KGB."

CHAPTER ELEVEN

Maria stood across the street and watched the two Americans, satisfaction nearly palpable. They'd fallen for the bait, and their next stop would be to their safe house—and Mickey's gang of sleepers. They would materialize out of the Russian landscape at the handler's beckoning. Fueled by his desperation to get Nadia safely home, Mickey would activate every agent on this side of the ocean.

And Maria would simply stand outside the door with a very large net.

This promised to be the biggest capture of Russian agents since they'd swept Moscow for friends of Oleg Rustikoff in 1962. And even then, Maria hadn't been able to receive the glory.

This time, Brezhnev would decorate his favorite double agent with the Star of Lenin.

And then, Maria's unrequited love would choke on the overwhelming if onlys. . . .

Yes, some betrayals were worth the price.

"What about Aranoff?" Mickey's breath sounded a good ten steps behind her—and labored. "What if they find him?"

"Keep up here, Jack, and I don't mean with your legs.

Engage that Mickey spy brain." Nadia glanced over her shoulder, glared at him as she raced through the entrance of the darkened outside market. She'd hidden Lena's Moscovitz on the other side of the two-acre plot of weeds, muddy trails, and the occasional cracked pavement held down by the metal shells of abandoned kiosks. She'd marked the place by the unforgettable odor of dead carp and pike churned up by the rain. "Aranoff is not on our side."

"How do you know he's not trying to help us?" Mickey protested.

"Yeah, and *what if he sent them?*" Nadia rounded on him, and he nearly plowed her over. He stopped short, breathing hard.

Did he think she enjoyed accusing one of her best friends of betrayal? That it didn't feel like a bowie knife turning in her stomach?

Mickey shook his head in denial, and the dark look he gave her pumped up her adrenaline another notch. She pounded her finger into his chest. "Sorry, but I'm not willing to wager your life on his loyalty. If you believe him so much, why did you follow me?" She raised her eyebrows, blinking away the water that ran into them. Fury had her heartbeat in overdrive, and she didn't care that every cell in her body felt soggy, that fatigue had turned her legs to kasha, and that she just wanted to curl into a ball and wake up in her living room in Nyack.

He stared at her. "You said you loved me."

That was it? The way to make Mickey come running? "I've said that before, Bub. What's the big deal?"

He swallowed, moved past her. "What if Aranoff is innocent?"

"Then I'll gladly be wrong. I'll do a jig across Red

Square. But until we know for sure, just follow me, okay?"

She cut down the stairs, then across the lower side of the market. Her foot sank into a puddle, a fresh dunking of acid-cold water up to her ankles. She felt wet to the bone, grimy, and downright frozen. And if Mickey didn't knock off the huffing behind her, and she wasn't referring to his ragged breathing, she just might have to let him run all the way to Pskov.

The market turned into little more than a graveyard of debris and foul smells at night, and with the drizzle, no one except a few hobos slept under the wooden countertops. She angled around the backside of a long wooden shelter, conveniently labeled "Reba" with a large ugly fish painted on the overhead sign. The Moscovitz sat where she'd left it, in a protected swaddling of fog and shadow.

She ran to the driver's door. Mickey edged up next to her, breathing hard. "I'm driving."

She couldn't help the incredulous look. "Get in the car." She opened the passenger door. "Stay low, and try not to get us killed."

He opened his mouth as if she'd landed a blow to his midsection. She ignored it and hopped in the driver's seat. The keys dangled from the ignition. One of the perks of communism: car theft was punishable by sure death in a Siberian gulag.

Stomping the clutch and the brake, she turned over the engine. It sputtered, lurched, died. Grinding her back teeth, she tried again.

Nothing but the rhythmic burp of an engine unable to engage.

"Want some help?" Mickey leaned forward, his hands on her seat, and she fought the desire to hit him.

"*Nyet.* I think I can start a car."

"Not if you're flooding the engine. Take your foot off the gas."

She looked down and bit back a retort when she moved her foot from the gas pedal to the brake.

Mickey said nothing as the car coughed, then turned over. She felt him lean back and could imagine the smile on his angular face, all sass and I-told-you-so.

She eased out of the market parking lot, across Lenin Street, and onto Pikorovsky Prospect. Streetlights pooled along the road, glistening against rain-soaked pavement. She flicked on the windshield wipers, and they screeched as they drew grimy lines across the glass. Gripping the wheel, she forced herself to drive slowly. Four-story apartments hovered over them, some with lighted windows, others black, like the ghosts of the Soviet Union watching the foreign invaders. She repressed a chill.

"Where are we going?" Mickey's voice emerged muffled, as if he were slouched in his seat.

"The safe house in Pskov."

"That's eight hours away. Do we have enough gas?"

Nadia glanced at the gauge, angry that Mickey was always one step ahead of her. The needle read half full. And in communist Russia, gas wasn't easily acquired. Even by party officials. "We'll get as far as we can."

"No, I have a better idea." The enthusiasm in his voice lit a spark of adrenaline, as if she needed any help for her heart to thump faster.

"What?" She turned onto Levsky Prospect, then again into a bank of garages, and cut the engine. They sat in silence. Rain dinged the car, and under her wool jacket, she shivered.

"We'll take the train."

She grimaced. "We tried that route, remember? KGB swarming the platform? Big ugly guys in black with guns under their jackets?"

"Looking like they might be expecting us? Yeah, I remember."

She stiffened, and the realization that Aranoff had given them the tickets felt like a sucker punch.

Mickey leaned forward, his arms folded over her seat, close and entirely too smug when he said, "So they won't think we'd try it again, right?"

She shook her head. "It's the most logical way to Pskov. Everyone rides the train."

"Except spies on the lam. I bet they have guards posted on every road out of Moscow. It just takes one overzealous brown boy, and we'll be facing the hot lights. If we're lucky."

He touched her hair, twirling it between his fingers, an old habit that turned her heart to mush.

"I saw in the paper that the circus was leaving in the morning for a tour of Estonia and Latvia." He leaned close, and his voice fell to a sweetly roughened whisper. "Have I ever told you I thought you'd make a great trapeze artist?"

"Mickey. . ."

"Scoot over. I'm driving." He got out of the car, and before she could protest, he'd opened her door. She growled as she climbed over the stick shift into the passenger seat but couldn't help the old fire in her stomach that made her remember the good old days: she and Mickey, two brains working in sync.

When he fired up the car and backed out, Nadia couldn't help but smile.

What was it about him that made her feel alive, even superhuman? As if she might indeed be able to fly through the air.

He needed her and depended on her. He saw her as his equal.

And after two years out of the loop—one of it feeling like a balloon, the second as if she'd somehow taken out her heart to wear on the outside of her body—she needed Mickey's confidence.

Yeah, she could be a trapeze artist. If he was holding onto the other bar, ready to catch her.

The Moscow Circus, a three-story coliseum with a million steps ringing its entrance onto Vernadsky Avenue, looked gloomy and uninspired as they pulled up to the back entrance. "I don't suppose you remember the time we sneaked Igor Khakhalev out of Russia."

Nadia shook her head, frowning. He noticed how drawn she looked, even in the wan light.

"Remember, he worked for the circus, doing concession sales? He was also a courier and would pass off information in the popcorn to his contacts."

Nadia shook her head. "Mickey, you're creative. I give you that."

His smile fell. That was about all he'd given her, wasn't it? Creativity and a daughter, and nothing in between. And she still *loved* him. He so didn't deserve it. The bigger question was, did she still trust him? He shrugged, hoping to deflect the guilt lodged in his chest. "Igor taught me a few tricks. The first being how to get inside the building."

He climbed out of the car and hunched his shoulders against the drizzle. Despite the heater pumping out its best supply, he felt like two-day-old kasha, gooey and gross. He heard Nadia's door slam, and she followed him through the puddles into an enclave of shadow. He pointed to a window, just above a huge wooden box of garbage. "The actors and custodians leave it open so they can use this place after hours."

"Won't they be here?"

He smiled and climbed up on the wooden box. "If they are, they won't wave their arms and scream for attention. Besides, a couple of Americans showing up to offer their endorsement certainly wouldn't upset their trading."

She smiled and hiked herself onto the box. Moscow was riddled with capitalistic hawkers, peddling everything from black-market jeans to outlawed music. The sins that plagued the communist gatekeepers looked downright tame against the turbulent backdrop of the last decade in America.

Mickey opened the window from the bottom. The frame creaked as it pivoted on its overhead hinges. He climbed in and straddled the sill, then reached down for her hand. She scaled the side and braced herself on the sill. As he climbed inside, she used his leverage to pull herself in.

Her agility always left him a little in awe. And disappointed. Couldn't she just need him a little? How could she love him yet not need him?

Nadia, the super spy, didn't need anyone. Ever. Which made loving her just a smidgen disappointing. She did nothing to quench his protective impulses, which roared to life when she walked into the room.

It left him feeling inadequate.

Sort of how he felt about his entire life.

He jumped down, then reached out to help her. She ignored his hand and jumped down with the grace of a leopard.

The place hadn't changed in the five-some years since he'd last combed the behind-stage labyrinth. Dark, cold, and creepy. Without a light, he could only make out lumps of darkness. He moved toward the middle of the corridor, brailled one hand down the far, stubbly cement wall, and held the other out for Nadia. She grabbed his arm, worked her way down to his hand, and held it.

Her hand felt soft and strong, and he tightened his grasp. They stumbled down the hall toward the dressing rooms, accompanied by nothing but the shuffle of their feet and the patter of rain on the street outside. The smell of dust and dampness saturated the place and left him feeling hollow and frozen. He'd caught some shut-eye in the car last night and on the train south this morning, but right now, he'd give about two years of his life for warm socks, a shower, and a fluffy bed with a wool blanket that went past his toes.

He wasn't going to go so far as to dream about Nadia sleeping beside him.

His hand trailed across a line in the wall, then up to an ancient round light switch. Common sense stopped him a second before he flicked it on. He kept trudging. The hope of warmth and, perhaps, a place to sleep outside the rain pushed him forward. They must be near the dressing rooms.

A puddle of light ran out from a doorway ahead, and he froze, listening past his heartbeat and the sound of Nadia breathing. Nothing. He moved closer, paused, finally worked his way to the door. He leaned into it, heard nothing. Slowly turning the handle, he eased it open.

Inside the dressing room, a red sofa, a black velvet overstuffed chair, and a lighted Formica dressing table beckoned him like a friend. He moved inside, pulling Nadia along with him, and closed the door. The place smelled of oils and body odor and the faintest hint of incense.

"What if they come back?" Nadia whispered, and he heard the panic in her voice despite her stoic expression.

He locked the door behind her and smiled.

She grinned at him, then walked past him and flopped on the overstuffed chair. "Where's room service?"

He was searching the cabinet under the dressing table. A bag of crackers, a can of herring, a sugar bowl, tea, jam, and a hunk of bread. "Right on."

He pulled out the fixings, sat on the sofa, and they made a sparse picnic on a small wooden table. Nadia ate the apricot jam Russian style—with a spoon. Her color returned slowly, and he realized how white, probably from cold, she'd been. She looked completely wrung out, circles bagging her beautiful eyes. Strands of her ginger brown hair spilled out of her black stocking cap, accentuating her high, nearly regal cheekbones. She ate with grace, and he felt like a boar next to her, diving into the bread like a man on death row.

Which, at the moment, didn't sound far from the truth.

"What next, Kimosabe?" she asked as she worked off a hunk of brown bread. His heart jumped at the old nickname. He'd called her the Lone Ranger once too often, and the comparison stuck.

He hadn't realized how much he'd enjoyed being her sidekick. He settled into the nickname, warmth rushing through him. "You miss this, don't you?"

Her smile fell. "At times."

He set down his teacup, aware that his fingers now smelled like herring. How appealing. He wiped them on a towel he found hanging over the doorknob. "Do you remember the time we impersonated the duchess and duke of Transylvania?" He easily conjured up the memory of her in a low-cut, rhinestone-trimmed dress, her ginger hair piled up on her head, a borrowed diamond necklace at her throat. He'd lost his heart all over again as he took her in his arms and swept her across the room.

A crooked smile creased her face. "Latvia. I remember. You nearly got us killed."

"Hey, it wasn't my idea to let you dance with General Malenkov. In fact, it nearly killed me, watching his meaty hands on you." He felt nauseous with the memory. The fact that she sat there, her legs pulled up, balancing her tea in her delicate, steady hands and grinning at him, didn't help his feelings of melancholy. Oh, how he'd missed her. She sipped her tea, mischief in her eyes.

"Yeah, you were so busy being jealous, you nearly tripped his office alarm." She giggled, and it swept his breath clear out of his chest. "I had to dance two extra songs just so you could tuck your brain back into your head."

"I can't help it if you are beautiful."

Her smile faded. "I don't feel so beautiful right now."

His voice dropped. "I think you are probably more beautiful this moment than I've ever seen you."

No, scratch that. If possible, she looked even better with her growing blush.

"Mickey, can I ask you something?" She didn't look at him, just stared at her tea. "Did you think of me in gulag?"

Her question felt like a one-two blow right in the gut. His voice even emerged winded. "Nadia, you are all I thought about. How I'd never see you again. How I'd hurt you. I felt sick with regret. All I hoped for was that I'd see you again."

She looked up, and the hope in her eyes felt palpable. It reached out to him and roped him. It was all he could do not to leap the table and pull her into his arms. He took a deep breath. "Sometimes, when things got especially bad, I'd think about our honeymoon or all those times we sat in Gregarin Park and talked about home. I'd envision riding horses with you or fooling around in the hay with you on your farm in New York." She worked at keeping a straight face, but one side of her mouth pulled up in a smile. Her eyes glistened as she stared again at her cup. "Sometimes I'd imagine taking you to Canton, showing you off to my mom and dad. I always regretted you not meeting them." He gave a wry laugh. "I had this running daydream of us riding through my hometown on a Harley, you hanging onto me, your long hair streaming out. I never did any time as a hippie and wondered if I'd missed my calling."

She laughed, and it sounded so sweet and full, it bathed all his wounded places. "Remember Berlin? You handled that motorbike pretty well."

"Yeah, I remember." He recalled her arms wrapped around his chest, her legs tight on his thighs as he took low turns, sirens screaming behind them. She'd laughed then, too. Oh, how he'd missed the thrill of being near her energy, feeding off her spunk. The silence between them felt thick and full of uncertainty.

"This is it, isn't it?"

She frowned, looked at him.

"The glory days are over, aren't they? You're not coming back."

She shook her head. "I can't be a mother and a spy."

Oh, yeah. They had a daughter. Her expression betrayed pain, her eyes searching his as if asking if he'd forgotten. He made a wry face. "Right. Sorry."

She ran her finger around her teacup. "Well, you've had a daughter for about six hours. I've had one for over a year. And even then, it's been. . .difficult to get used to." She looked away. "I admit that half the time I don't know what I'm doing. I keep wondering if I'm going to make a huge mistake that messes her up for life. It's like I'm walking into this dark tunnel, just hoping and praying we make it to the other side. I'll tell you, it's a lot scarier than running from the KGB." She smiled wryly, still not meeting his eyes. "I do miss being here, running the game with you. But something inside me changed when Ekaterina was born. I changed." She looked up, and a tear hung off her beautiful lashes. "I just want to be a good mother. And a mother never forgets her child."

He felt like a jerk and caught her hand. "Neither does a good father. I won't forget again."

Her gaze touched his, and in it, hope felt hot and real. He swallowed back a wave of desire. What was he doing here with her? Planning a run for the border with a circus crew? Yep, he was a first-class clown. He should be back at the factory, meeting with Aranoff, plotting her escape and his recovery of his postcards, his evidence of a job well done.

Only, what job was that exactly? He'd save a nation. . . for the good of eternity? But he'd sacrifice his family in the exchange. He had started his clandestine career with a vivid belief God had directed him into service. But that vision had faded in clarity over the last twenty-four hours. His brain felt webbed, his future as dark as moonless sky.

What, exactly, did God want of him anymore?

He pulled his hand away and reached for his cup, swirled the tea, then drank it down. The spicy liquid went straight to his weary bones and fortified his resolve to keep her at a distance, to get her home safely. "Tell me, why do you suspect Aranoff?"

His tone changed to business, another attempt to get a handle on his feelings, focus his goals instead of taking her in his arms and further snarling this mess.

Her slight smile, the one that appeared when he touched her hand, faded.

He sighed.

She leaned back, her hands folded on her lap. "He had the postcards. Lena came back after you left and showed them to me."

His hopes took a soaring leap. "You have them?"

She nodded, reached inside her jacket, and pulled out his postcards. The ones he'd sent her from Kazakhstan. The ones with answers. "I haven't read them, well, not all of them. But a few. . ." Her expression turned raw and vulnerable, and it did devastating things to his pulse rate. "Your writing is very romantic."

He closed his eyes. He'd meant every word, but suddenly he felt sick that he'd used love letters to his wife to prove his innocence.

"I meant every word." He opened his eyes but couldn't look at her. Not now.

"I know. That's why I had to come after you. I always trusted you, Mickey. Even when you were just my handler, somehow I knew you'd be there, that you cared about me, even if you couldn't show it."

He couldn't look at her. Sure, he'd hidden his feelings for her for about two-point-three seconds. And that was only because she was the daughter of the great Edward Neumann. He should have probably tried harder.

"You were always my rock. My solid ground. The voice of reason in my wild, sometimes crazy brain." She shook her head, memories in her eyes. "And then, after a while, I started hoping you'd be there when I got back and that your eyes would light up as if you missed me. I was crazy in love with you long before I thought you knew I existed. And your postcards reminded me why. Because through all the layers of camouflage, you loved me. And that is what brought me home, every time. That's what brought me back to Russia."

He wanted to wince. Oh great, another nail in his coffin. Why didn't he write about the weather? "You should have obeyed me, Nadia. We have a daughter at home who needs you."

"She needs you, too."

He glanced at the postcards. *She needs you, too.* Heat, the kind of warmth that comes with the hope of family and tomorrows started to simmer in his chest. "Can I see them?"

She handed the package to him. He took one, looked it over. "I wonder why Aranoff had them."

"Hello? Doesn't that bother you in the least?"

He looked at her, rocked by her frown. "No. He has access to my box. He must have been hiding them."

Nadia's frown deepened. "My gut tells me he's up to something."

He handed the pile of cards back to Nadia. "Keep

them in a safe place until this is over."

"You don't want them?"

"Not yet. If the KGB finds me, I don't want them to find the cards."

She paled and tucked the bundle back into her jacket. "Lena thinks Aranoff has been a double for years."

Mickey leaned back against the sofa far enough so that his hands couldn't reach out on their own and touch her. He shook his head. "No. He had enough information to corrupt and destroy our entire network years ago. Why wait? Besides, he's passed off enough secrets to make himself vulnerable."

"Or not. Did those secrets pan out?"

Mickey traced back time, to places, events, people. "Most of them."

Nadia frowned. Then she took off her hat and shook out her hair. Slightly damp, it hung in waves around her face. He made fists on his up-drawn knees. *Stay away, Mickey. You don't want to leave her with* two *children,* two *mouths to feed after you've been killed.*

He gulped a deep breath, and his brain formed around another, more devastating scenario. "What about Lena?" It physically hurt to even say her name, as if fire blew through his lungs.

"Lena?"

He licked his lips, forced out his thoughts. "She knew where we went tonight, right? Knew you took her car. What if she followed us?"

Nadia nodded, and he saw her working out his words behind those beautiful eyes.

"For that matter, she didn't seem surprised to see me. As if she knew I'd—we'd—show up."

Nadia slowly nodded. "And she was gone for a long time today. In fact, she was the one who suggested we go to the Pskov safe house."

Mickey stared at her, his worst fears boiling in his chest. One of his best friends, his best agents, could be a traitor. Right under his nose. Had either Lena or Aranoff been a part of his betrayal to the KGB? The thought burned like a blow low in his gut.

"I gotta get you safely home," Mickey said slowly.

Nadia leaned forward. "Ditto."

He opened his mouth to protest, but she held up a finger and gave him a warning look. "Sometimes you just gotta trust your wife, Mickey. After all, you were the one who liked to quote Proverbs 31, remember?" She narrowed her eyes at him and unfortunately remembered his words too well. "Who can find a virtuous woman, her price is far above rubies. The heart of her husband *doth safely trust* in her and she will do him good and not evil all the days of her life." She looked way too cute when she knew she was right. "It's time to hang up your spy hat and come home. Kat needs you." Her eyes glistened. "I need you."

If he had any hopes of resisting her, of not taking her in his arms, they died right there. Almost against his will, he reached out. "Hope," he heard himself say, and it sounded more like a moan, a long buried pain that could no longer be stifled. His eyes burned as she came willingly into his embrace.

He kissed her without a thought for what might be tomorrow, tightening his hold on her as if afraid she might just dissolve and he'd awaken in a dingy, freezing cell, this moment nothing but an agonizingly sweet memory.

"I love you, Nadia," he said and heard her intake of

breath as he kissed her again. Yes, the glory days had died. But their passion lived. And somehow, with her in his arms, he could imagine a future. Someplace unscarred by duty and country. Someplace where he could drink her smell, taste her sweet tears, and love her like he had in his dreams.

"And I love you, Mickey," she said as she pulled away, and he saw her words in her eyes. "I always will."

As he tucked her back into his arms, closing his mind to anything but right now—this safe place where he might embrace hope—he knew he didn't deserve the sweet love of the woman who saw through him to his heart and wouldn't let him die.

CHAPTER TWELVE

Mickey thrived on the difficult tasks. The ones that threatened to one-two flatten him, when he had to gasp in air and courage to survive. Like braving a Siberian-cold night in his cell. Or sneaking into a Kazakhstani missile compound dressed as a scientist and smuggling out pictures that would alert the world to Soviet lies.

But this felt so easy, it rocked his confidence. So easy that the tiny hairs had raised on the back of his neck and his sixth spy sense sounded like the bells of St. Basil's.

He and Nadia had simply slipped into the unsuspected garb of animal handlers, complete with green padded pants and jackets, matching stocking caps, and a little carefully smudged dirt across their cheeks, and all they'd had to do was carry a small battalion of toy poodles onto the train, hide behind the crates of costumes, and suddenly they found themselves, midafternoon, staring at the swells of a wheat field outside Pskov.

They'd ditched the train at Smolensk station after a semi-heated debate about staying on beyond Pskov to Estonia.

Nadia still believed Lena innocent of blame, despite Mickey's summation of the facts—something that irked him more than he wanted to admit. Wasn't it Nadia, who, two days ago, accused Lena of being his mistress? The fact that she wanted to stake their lives on the same woman's information felt like. . .a Gloria Steinem edict. Women of today, unite.

Women. And it didn't help that Nadia looked even more devastatingly beautiful in the garb of laborer, her long black wig pulled back in a white handkerchief. Dirt stained her high cheekbones, and it was all he could to do keep his focus on looking out for trouble and off of her—aka trouble with a capital C. H.: Crazy Hope.

Infectious Crazy Hope. Igniting all sorts of dreams.

Sometime between the wee hours of the night and the dawn, with her nestled in his arms, he knew he was headed home. Nadia had sketched the little girl's picture in his mind with her stories of Kat's birth, her first steps, her lopsided smile. He couldn't wait to meet his daughter. The idea of being a father made him feel whole. Clean. Loved.

Who can find a virtuous woman? For her price is far above rubies. The heart of her husband doth safely trust in her and she will do him good and not evil all the days of her life. Oh, wow, did he understand that. If only she knew how much he wanted to trust her, believe in her love. Like air, she surrounded him, kept his heart beating, the blood flowing in his veins.

Yes, he'd head straight back to America—right after he dragged his betrayer through the doors of the CIA.

After disembarking, they hitched a ride with a fellow laborer hauling the last potato crop into Pskov. The thin man with sunken cheeks, a grizzled beard, and work-worn hands leered at Nadia so many times, Mickey thought he might have to bump him out of the truck. Thankfully, by the time sunset simmered over the far sky, the worker let them off just outside the city. Naked birch trees fractured the orange sky, and the nip of winter chilled the air. Nadia walked with her hands in her pockets, her boots kicking up dust, the wind tangling that long black hair.

They startled a pheasant. It flew up, out, and dragged with it memories of hunting with his family in Ohio. A smile tugged at Mickey's lips.

"What's so funny?"

Nadia had glanced at him and managed to capture the sunset in her eyes, turning them pure gold. She wore the smallest hint of a smile, as if she could read his mind, the little spy, and he realized that it didn't hurt at all.

No, in fact, it felt. . .healing. He suddenly wondered why he'd spent so much energy over the past two days walling her out.

"I was thinking about my dad. Hunting with him on the farm. We used to go out every Thanksgiving, see if we could bag a deer or maybe a wild turkey."

"I look forward to meeting him."

The thought of Nadia inside her father's massive embrace dredged up an unfamiliar, soft feeling. He nodded, unable to speak.

"I wish you had the same relationship with my dad."

Mickey betrayed his feelings in a grunt, and when she sighed, he felt immediately sorry. It wasn't her fault her father didn't want her to marry a man who lived a life of deceit. For the first time, he glimpsed the reasons why.

Perhaps Edward didn't want her to love a man who followed in his footsteps. A man who left her when she needed him most. "Your dad has every reason to hate me."

"He doesn't hate you. He just. . .well, you weren't his first pick of husbands." She looked over and winked, looking so beautiful he wanted to drop to his knees and beg her to run away with him. To Europe. Maybe the Black Forest. Or Switzerland.

Oh yeah, Ekaterina.

No, he'd go back to New York where Edward Neumann waited to hound his every step. He glanced at Nadia, at that beautiful smile, those eyes that told him she trusted him and suddenly knew she was worth every moment he spent living under Edward's scrutiny. Dodging his disdain.

"I'm sorry I never brought Ekaterina to meet your parents, Mickey. I. . .didn't know if you told them we were married. And after you left, I didn't know what to think."

She meant she didn't know if he would return. If he still loved her. He couldn't help but feel pain deep inside his chest.

"Do you think. . .your mother will like me?" Nadia didn't look at him as she kicked out a rock. He watched it roll into the ditch.

"Are you kidding? She'll adore you." He bumped her with his elbow, and she grinned up at him. But the longing in her face shook him. Realization spread through him like a hot breath. "That's right. You never had a mother."

She shrugged, looked away, and shook her head. "Grandma filled in the gaps. Sorta. But I always wondered what it might be like to have a mother. Someone who sat on my bed at night, combed my hair, listened to my woes about the boys in school."

"There were boys at your school?" he teased softly, and she gave him a mock glare.

"You know what I mean."

"Well, my mother never sat on my bed combing my hair, but I do agree my life was richer for her patience, for her dedication to our family. She was always there after school with frosted graham crackers or homemade cookies, and boy could she cook a Sunday roast."

She grimaced. "What is it with men that they associate mothers with food?"

"What else is there in life?"

She grinned, but sadness touched her eyes.

He stopped, suddenly realizing that he'd let the bull moose in him run roughshod over her feelings. He touched her arm as she walked out ahead of him. "I'm sorry. I guess I've never thought about not having a mother. She's always been there, like a part of my life that is solid and good and warm. Sometimes she's in my head, reminding me of things I'd learned or precepts she tried to teach me. Sometimes she's just in my heart, smiling. My mother made me who I am, I suppose. She gave me any kindness and patience I might possess."

Nadia's eyes filled. "That's exactly the kind of mother I want to be."

He ran his finger along her cheek, moved at the image of her loving Ekaterina the way his mother loved him. "You will be, *maya doragaya.*"

She blushed, and he felt something inside him turn weak. "We'd better hurry. If we prowl the streets after dark, they may think we're spies or something."

"Right," she said, and thankfully, she turned before he could act on the desire to pull her into his arms.

The wind rustled the leaves of the trees, bringing with it the smell of coal smoke. Pskov had grown over the years to a town of twelve thousand, but the majority of the inhabitants lived in the outskirts in communities of poverty. Rutted dirt roads angled off the main thoroughfare, pushing apart row after row of dilapidated blue- or green-painted shacks, two-room hovels with outhouses and water pumps in the front yard. An occasional milking cow ambled down the road or roamed the yards ringed by lopsided fences. The sound of chickens punctuated the air.

Mickey reached down and found Nadia's hand. It was cold, and he held it tight, tucking it into his own pocket.

Yeah, he was going home. He had the postcards; they would declare his innocence. He'd find his betrayer and hop the first transport stateside. And as for his life of adventure, well, somehow he'd figure out a way to be the hero reflected in Nadia's eyes. Maybe it would be enough.

He ignored the niggle of doubt as they turned down a side street, ambling like a married couple returning from a hard day at work, and found Volgaskaya #10, just another shack among the thousands. The Pskov safe house.

They shuffled to the end of the street in silence, then rounded the corner, kept their heads down, and trudged down the alley. Mickey swayed, just slightly, affecting a Russian after-work stupor.

Two chickens in the yard, some feed ground into the cold soil, and a water jug outside the side door—the only door to the house—evidenced an attempt to blend. Mickey wondered at the surveillance and hoped that, if anyone waited inside, they'd ask questions before they shot him.

The errant fear that Lena had truly double-crossed them and sent thugs ahead grabbed him by the throat. He tensed as he crept up the walk. "Wait."

He put Nadia behind him and cracked open the door. It whined on its hinges. Nothing. His heart lodged in his ribs, he entered, wishing he had his Russian Makarov or even the agency-issued Colt .38.

The entry hall led into a small kitchen. A hunk of brown bread on the table, a pile of smoked salmon, two bowls of borscht, a container of *smeytana,* and the smell of steam in the air made him freeze, whirl, and stalk down the hall. He had Nadia by the arm when they jumped him.

"No!"

He landed on his chin. He blinked back pain between his eyes as he rolled. He struck out blindly. "Nadia, run!"

Another cuff across his face. Then a bag over his head, shutting out the dim light. He heard Nadia scream as he was hauled to his feet, dragged back to the kitchen, and thrown to the floor. "Nadia!" He clawed at the mask, but a knee into his back pinned him to the ground. He felt his arm wrenched backward, his hand forced back in a military-style hold. Pain shot up his arm, pummeled his brain.

"Nadia!" He closed his eyes and waited for the blows to begin.

"Daddy, no!"

Edward Neumann, age fifty-plus, six-foot-two, still had the build of a twenty-year-old OSS agent. The fact that he now straddled Mickey, his knee pasting Mickey's backbone to the floor, didn't bode well for the future relationship of her father and her husband. Nadia jumped on Edward, one arm around his neck, pulling him back. "No! Leave him alone."

Edward grasped his daughter's arm. "Let me go, Hope. Mickey is a traitor to everyone, including you. Stay out of this." He nodded to an agent dressed in workman's clothes, who moved to relieve him. The agent pinned Mickey's neck to the ground with a white grip. Nadia wanted to scream.

"Get off me, Hope," Edward repeated, and this time weariness etched his tone.

Nadia's heart thudded in her throat as she released him. He backed off Mickey, turned, and she dredged up every morsel of courage as she stared at him with her best death-ray look.

He didn't flinch. Her father always had the ability to knock someone to their knees with a look, and it had taken Nadia years of self-talk to both see beyond his fierceness to the love inside and stand up to him when he tried his weapons on her. She hadn't been the daughter of a spymaster without learning his tricks. She lifted her chin and refused to budge. "Hi ya, Dad. Welcome to Russia."

"Don't you 'Welcome to Russia' me!" He shot a look at Mickey, fighting like a badger to writhe out of the take-down grasps of the CIA babysitters. Edward motioned with his head toward the next room. The one with the closed door. Nadia gulped, but she fought for control. She didn't care what it cost her—her father wouldn't hurt a hair on Mickey's head.

Edward rounded on her. "Do you know how worried I've been? Your grandmother is beside herself, not to mention your daughter! She keeps asking for Mommy, and I don't have an answer." He combed a hand through his salt-and-pepper hair. "What were you thinking?"

"Oh, I don't know, perhaps trying to save my husband from execution?" she snapped.

He glared at her while the agents dragged a snarling Mickey into the next room. Nadia smiled to see that he got in at least two bone-crunching kicks. It took all her resolve not to jump her fellow agents and help him.

"Don't remind me that you married that. . .that. . .traitor. Did you forget that he cheated on you? That he demolished your so-called wedding vows?"

She trembled with rage as she stared at her father. His deep green eyes, normally filled with compassion, even hunger, now blazed with unbridled anger. She steeled herself. "He's not a traitor. He didn't betray me. He loves me, Dad."

The man went from red to white in an instant. He scowled at her, as if trying to get a fix on the woman she'd become, then shook his head and paced past her. Mickey's growls, somewhat muffled, punctuated the silence from behind the closed door, and the gray fingers of the approaching night pressed against the shadows, giving the room a gloomy, chilly feel. Her weary legs wanted to collapse, send her with a thud to the frayed brown carpet. But she tightened her fists in her pockets, steadied herself, turned, and watched her father's wide shoulders shake.

"Why did you have to come here, Nadia? I thought we'd talked about this. You were going to give up this. . . stupidity." He turned, and fatigue showed in his eyes. "This is no life for a mother. Or a woman." He shook his head, crossed his arms, and sighed. "I should have never let you join the company. What was I thinking?"

Her heart felt strangely heavy. She glanced at the closed door. "Has it ever occurred to you that I might be just like you?"

He frowned. A muscle twitched in his jaw. Her voice softened, and a strange warmth welled up inside her. So different from the desperation that fueled her adrenaline for years, this warmth felt more like empathy. Like acceptance.

"Dad, I just wanted to do something important with my life, too. I wanted to make you proud."

He swallowed, and for a man who spent years figuring out how to hide his emotions, he did a poor job of not letting them streak across his face. It fortified Nadia's courage. "Daddy, I love you. And I'm sorry that you were worried about me. But I'm all grown up now, and I get to make my own decisions. Yes, I'm a mother, and I plan to return home to Ekaterina and do my best to be a good mother to her. But I'm also a wife. Mickey's wife. I'm sorry that hurts you. But I'm going to do everything I can to clear his name. And it starts with me telling you that Mickey loves me. He didn't cheat on me with Lena or anyone else." She reached inside her jacket. "I even have proof."

She pulled out the bundle of postcards and held them out. "They're love letters. From Kazakhstan, sent during his mission. Every one speaks of his devotion to me. How he misses me. What he hopes for when he returns. That hardly sounds like a man who loves another woman."

Edward stared at the bundle, an odd look in his eyes. "He sent you postcards from Kazakhstan?" He took the bundle, cracked open the brown paper, then pulled out a card and sat down at the rough-hewn table. "Hope, can you hand me that pack of cigarettes from my jacket?"

Nadia stared at him. "Since when do you smoke?"

He looked up and gave her a look that reminded her, again, how little she knew about this man who had nurtured and raised her like he might be a farmer from upstate New York. Even working under his thumb for ten years had revealed little in the way of his activities. To her, he'd always be larger than life, immoveable, and the foundation for her definition of hero. With a trembling hand, she reached into his leather jacket, hung over the back of a chair at the kitchen table, and handed him the pack of *Pytor Ones.* He tapped one out, broke it open, and pulled out a tiny magnifier, a miniature viewing device. He rolled it between two fingers and grinned at her like a ten-year-old.

She lowered herself into a chair, completely baffled.

Taking out a knife from a sheath at his ankle, he took out one of Mickey's postcards, turned it over, and began to work up the edge of the stamp. Nadia braced her arms on the table, hearing Mickey's occasional threats. She wondered how the thugs in the next room were able to hold him down. He sounded like he could rip the heart out of a bear.

Edward peeled back the stamp, then held it up. A small black dot, about one millimeter round centered in the middle of the stamp. "Mickey, Mickey. Isn't he the clever one? He certainly knows his tradecraft." He placed the stamp down on the table, black dot up and, putting the microscope to his eye, leaned over for a closer look at the speck.

Nadia's pulse swelled in her ears. "Is that a microdot?" In short, a mini-photograph, it condensed information into a form that would be overlooked by censors. She'd seen them concealed in coins, rings, and even slit into the sides of postcards. She suddenly felt like an idiot.

Edward looked up, smiled. "Your husband just might be telling the truth."

Nadia pounced to her feet, stalked across the room, and slammed open the door to the next room. Mickey lay on his back, his mask wadded around his mouth, and as she entered, he landed a brain-stunning blow to the man trying to pin him.

"Let him go!" Nadia yelled. She advanced into the

room and, by the expressions on the faces of his assailants, had blood in her eyes. They frowned at her, then released their hold on Mickey and backed up. She felt like a hero as she knelt over Mickey and yanked the mask off his head. He stared at her, confused, then his gaze went past her to the door. She followed it.

Oh, yeah, she was a real hero. Edward filled the doorframe, eyebrows up, shaking his head at the guards. "Let him go, boys. I want to hear this story."

CHAPTER THIRTEEN

Nadia sat at the worn wooden table, watching her two men tear apart a pile of smoked salmon and down Russian Kvas, and she knew, without a doubt, why she'd married Mickey.

He was a shorter, wilder version of her father. He had the same fierce eyes, the identical determined set of his russet-whiskered jaw, and a patriotism that reverberated off him like the smell of masculinity. And they both had a protective streak that left her just a little weak. Mickey had struggled out of his bonds, pounced to his feet, and put her behind him like she might be in some sort of danger.

It had taken all of Edward's savvy and negotiation skills to talk Mickey into staying put and not fleeing with his bride to Siberia, where no one—not even his own countrymen—might find him.

Not that Nadia blamed him, the way Edward sized Mickey up with those narrowed green eyes like he might be a KGB mole.

However, after briefing their former chief-of-station of their activities over the past forty-eight hours while Edward peeled off two more stamps from Mickey's postcards, the gleam in Edward's eye sharpened to pure, begrudging respect.

"So you sent out copies of your film to your PO box,"

Edward summed up as he sat at the kitchen table, downing a midnight snack. He tore off a hunk of salty red meat from a piece of salmon skin. He followed with a bite of black bread. Nadia's stomach churned, watching them. Oh, great, now Mickey would smell like smoked fish when he kissed her.

She hid a smile. Yeah, she was going to figure out a way to get back inside those arms. Especially after falling asleep in them last night. She'd expected more. . .after all, he hadn't seen her for two years. Still, the sweetness of his simple affection had ignited a blaze inside her, one that she fully intended to feed to inferno. Oh, how she loved this man. She loved his passion for the truth, the fear that edged his eyes whenever they worked together, the way he depended on her strength, her ability to fend for herself. She especially loved his tenderness, the way he twirled her hair around his fingers, and his protective urges, especially when he could barely protect himself.

If she harbored any lingering fears about the man she'd loved and admired having been crushed under the vices of gulag, they died as Mickey triumphantly summed up his past two years to her father, his boss. Still, hearing how he was tortured ripped out her heart, and agony added to pain when he cleared his throat and admitted that his two best agents, and friends, might have turned on him.

"I don't know who to suspect," Mickey said with a glance at her. He had the most beautiful green eyes, piercing and rich, and for a moment, she couldn't help but compare them to Aranoff's. Pale blue, even weak. Anger flared inside her at what the weasel had done to her husband. The memory of Mickey stripped to his shorts and shivering in her backseat still left her wanting to howl.

Thankfully, his bruised lip had vanished, and the black eye blended with the rest of the tough laborer look. In two days, he'd gone from heart wrenching to heart breaking.

And if she played her cards right, she'd get to take him home like a souvenir. No, he hadn't changed his tune, but the way she'd seen their daughter's image outlined in his eyes, she knew. Mickey's heart was already turned toward home. Perhaps he'd even abandon his quest for his betrayers. He hadn't mentioned going after Lena or Aranoff once since last night.

God's mercies overwhelmed her. The Almighty had answered her desperate pleas, helped her break Mickey free from gulag, protected them, and had given her and her daughter back the man they loved. *"Lo, I am with you always, even unto the end of the world."*

An unfamiliar warmth washed over her as the teakettle whistled behind her. She rose to grab a hot pad and move it off the burner of the coal stove. The cement coal stove engulfed half the kitchen and spat out heat for the house, devouring the smell of mold and exhaling coal smoke.

Black crud lined the walls, graying the whitewashed paint above a shoulder-high line of grimy mint green. Nadia wouldn't be surprised if they all left the place with bacteria spores breeding in their lungs. She already felt infested, with dirt imbedded in her pores. She must be a real beauty dressed in dirty green army pants, a striped white and blue sailor's shirt, and matted, sweaty hair. It took all her courage to catch her reflection in the window. Yep, it sent a wash of terror through her.

Better not to look. She poured out three cups of tea and passed them over to the table.

"Frankly, my bets are on Lena," Mickey said as he took

the cup. "She knew I was back in town. After I returned from Kazakhstan, I contacted her twice, hoping to find out where Nadia had moved to." He didn't look at her. "I thought she'd moved in with a friend."

Edward put down his bread and wiped his fingers with a napkin. "You didn't consider that she'd returned to America?"

Mickey shook his head. "I suspected that she wasn't happy with me. I never knew that she was pregnant."

Nadia watched her father's reaction, saw the doubt flicker in his eyes. "So Lena knew you were back in town."

Mickey leaned back on his chair, balancing it on two legs as he parked it against the wall. Inside the tiny kitchen, the grimy overhead light gave little cheer, barely scraping away the darkness that pushed through the windows. Outside, the night wind had begun to howl, warning of a storm. Nadia rubbed her arms, feeling gooseflesh rise. Having removed her wig, she longed for a hot bath and a warm bed and one of Grandma Grape's homemade quilts.

"Yes. I had arranged to meet her at *Zhenshina Belaya Nocha,* a nightclub in town. When I arrived, she didn't show. Aranoff was there, and he told me to meet him back at the safe house. I admit I was tired. I'd been running all over the city, and I laid down. When I awoke, it was to a small welcoming committee of KGB regulars." He shot Nadia a quick look. "They weren't especially gentle, and the first memory I have after that is waking up in a cell in Lubyanka. It gets less pretty from there."

He blew out a breath and lowered the chair to all four legs, then folded his hands on the table. Nadia reached out and grabbed his hand, threading her fingers into his grip. His hands always felt warm, strong, safe. Today they were also rough. He squeezed her hand.

"According to my sources, you gave out the names of Wilson and Sukharov." Edward's voice betrayed no indictment. A practiced feat, Nadia guessed.

A vein throbbed in Mickey's jaw. "No. I didn't."

Edward frowned. He picked up the knife, speared a pickle off the plate. "So who did?"

Silence competed with Nadia's heartbeat. She met Mickey's gaze and saw in it pain. "I don't know. Lena maybe. She knew Wilson and Sukharov."

"As did Aranoff," said Nadia, suddenly wondering why she felt the urge to protect Lena. What if the sparrow had betrayed them all?

Except, Lena *had* masterminded their escape to the safe house. Wouldn't she have sent her Russian cohorts on their trail also? The fact that Mickey and Edward sat in this semi-warm kitchen unscathed seemed solid proof of Lena's innocence.

Both Edward and Mickey stared at Nadia, eyebrows high. She shrugged. "Well, I did tell him that I was pregnant and asked him to pass on the news to Mickey." She looked pointedly at her husband. "He didn't tell you, did he?"

"He didn't have time." Mickey shook his head. "He took a great risk in meeting me at the club. I still can't figure out how they found his safe house, but I am sure it was compromised after that."

"I used it," Nadia said, "when I got here. Aranoff arranged for me to meet him there, just like he had you."

Mickey frowned. "Well, maybe he didn't know it had been compromised. Maybe Lena clued them in—"

"And didn't tell him? He's her cousin."

"Yeah, and a double! You don't think that she'd earn about a thousand medals for netting him? Good thing she didn't know you were here until we arrived at her house."

Nadia stared at him, memory rousing in the back of her brain. "She did know I was here," she said slowly. "I saw her at the nightclub. *Zhenshina Belaya Nocha.* She left right before I met up with Aranoff."

Mickey swallowed, licked his lips. She noticed that his grip on her hand had tightened. "So, it's a safe bet she knew you were going to rescue me."

Nadia felt cold radiating from thc inside out. "That's a safe bet."

"Enough to convince her KGB conspirators at the Gorkilov Prison to let me go?"

Nadia frowned, scrolling back time. "No, how can that be? I bribed one of the guards. Well, I mean Aranoff bribed the guards."

"What if the guard was already planning on freeing Michael?" Edward asked, cradling his teacup in his hand. "You and Aranoff may have played right into his hands."

Nadia massaged her temple with her fingers. "I don't know. I just know that Mickey is free, and we have to get out of here." She looked up into Mickey's beautiful eyes, willing herself to see agreement there. "Right?"

Mickey met her gaze, and what she saw in it sent her heart crashing to her knees. Not agreement. Not even anger.

Revenge.

"No, Mickey, please."

"Nadia, she betrayed us. She sent two men to their deaths. She destroyed a year of our lives." Mickey's voice turned harsh. "How can you not want me to repay her?"

Nadia shook her head, her eyes burning. "Don't be a fool, Mickey. How can you expect any less from her? She's your enemy. You knew that going in."

A muscle pulled in his jaw, and realization hit her like a slap.

"Wait. Please tell me that this doesn't have anything to do with any. . .feelings you have for her." Her throat felt raw, and she gulped back a sickened taste of betrayal. "No, Mickey, please."

His anger visibly crumbled, and he reached out, touched her cheek, oblivious of her father sitting across from them. "No, Nadia. Nothing like that. I promise." His own eyes reddened. "I'm just angry at everything we lost. This isn't over. Lena needs to be brought to justice."

She cupped her hand over his, wove her fingers between his. "If you stay here, they'll catch you."

He swallowed, looked down, sucked in a deep breath. And suddenly she realized what she'd been demanding from him. Not just his heart—but his soul. His very reason for living. He'd spent his entire life building a web of protection for the America he loved—she loved—and now she asked him to surrender it all. For her. He looked up at her and confirmed the truth in his tortured gaze.

She couldn't hold onto a man like Mickey. Yes, he was just like her father. Agonizingly so. Mickey would never be happy living on the farm in upstate New York or even at an analyst's desk in Washington. What had she been thinking?

Mickey belonged in Russia. He spoke the language. He ate the food. He even looked like a Russian with his stubble of beard and work-worn hands.

But she couldn't stay. Not with Ekaterina waiting. She, too, had a purpose in life. If she wanted a real marriage with Mickey Moore, she'd have to trust God to figure out how to make it work.

Maybe marrying him had been a mistake after all.

She closed her eyes, willing herself to make the right decision.

"You're right, Mickey. You have my blessing to stay here and save the world."

Mickey died a little inside as Nadia rose from the table, grabbed her coat, and strode outside.

Nothing but the smell of the fish, the tea, and his own failures, screaming in the silence, remained. He half-rose to run after her, but Edward's hand on his arm stopped him. "Wait. She needs some time."

Mickey ripped out of Edward's grasp. "Right. Like you'd be at all unhappy for her to go home alone." He braced both hands on the table and glared at Edward. "You've been dreaming of this day since we met. Your greatest hope is that Nadia will wake up and boot me out of her life."

Edward's jaw twitched, but he met Mickey's gaze. "I want her to be happy."

"Yeah, well guess what? Me, too." Mickey stalked away from the table, amazed at the anger that boiled in his chest. Twenty-four hours ago, he'd have been thrilled at Nadia's announcement: Go, save the world, with my blessing. Yeah, like he believed that, but at least she'd said it and without a hint of sarcasm.

As if she meant it. As if she might be too hurt to fight him any longer.

His chest tightened. She didn't actually believe again the idea that he'd been unfaithful? *Please, no.* He rounded on Edward, needing a place to put his anger. "I haven't done much right since I married Nadia, but I do know that marrying her was the one good thing I've done in my life. She loves me, Neumann, whether you like it or not."

"I'm just trying to protect her." Edward had found his feet, his voice low and very dangerous. Mickey ignored it.

"Yeah, well, that's my job."

"Hardly. No, I was the one charged with protecting her, and—"

"You've done a groovy job, pal," Mickey finished. He stepped up, a hair away from Edward. His voice dropped. "Did it ever occur to you that you are the one she needs protecting from?"

Edward's mouth opened, as if Mickey had sucker-punched him. Mickey nodded viciously. "That's right. Can't you see that everything she's ever done is to get your attention? It's so obvious." Mickey shook his head, pacing the kitchen. "The night we were at the Winter Ball in Leningrad, didn't you see her check to see if you were looking when we snuck into Pashov's office? And afterwards, she practically marched into your office with the negatives."

"I wasn't there," Edward snapped. "How could I know?"

"Exactly my point, boss. You. Weren't. There." Mickey stopped pacing, glared at him. "Do you know how many stories she's told me about waiting for you to return from one of your many disappearances? You missed every major event in her life. First day of first grade, the year she won the state spelling bee, senior prom. No wonder she moved to Russia. She was just trying to get close to you." He hadn't realized that his voice had climbed back to the higher decibels. He fought to lower it and realized he was shaking. Edward just stared at him, wide-eyed.

"If anyone needs to protect her, it's me!" He thumped his chest. "And by the way, if you didn't happen to notice. . . the woman doesn't really need protecting. She does pretty well on her own. In fact, she scares me right out of my skin half the time."

Edward swallowed. "Well, we have that in common."

Mickey's mouth opened, and for a moment his words stumbled. He sucked in a hot breath. "Listen, I can appreciate your dedication to the job. Everyone can see that you're driven as if on some secret mission to rid the world of the communist curse. But I love Nadia, and I am not going to let you destroy our lives."

Edward held up his hands in surrender, his eyes dark as, behind them, he battled for the right words. "I admit I didn't want her falling for you, Michael. I don't want her to get hurt. I know you're married to the job, and I just don't want to see her become a widow."

Mickey closed his eyes. "She won't be. After I finish this job, I'm going back to her."

"Yeah. Sure," Edward said, his face suddenly tired, suddenly betraying his years of sacrifice, of living with lies. "That's what I said."

Mickey stared at him, his brain way too tired to figure out Edward's meaning. The older man sat wearily on his chair. "Believe me when I tell you that the best revenge you can enact on Lena or Aranoff is to get your microdots out of Russia. The United States Navy needs the information on the ocean surveillance satellites." He cast a look at the closed door. Mickey had to wonder how far Nadia had gone and, indeed, if he should find her. It occurred to him that the old, sassy Nadia might have stood her ground, demanded her way. This new Nadia, the one with patience, guts, and depth, turned his brain and heart into hard little knots.

He sat and cradled his head in his hands. He smelled

like fish. So much for his hope of finding a quiet place with Nadia and trying to rekindle their old romance. After last night, the way she'd relaxed in his embrace, he'd conjured up a pretty vibrant recollection of their wedding night. It had left him trembling, and it took all his self-control to let her sleep, peace painted on her beautiful face. If it were possible, she had become even more beautiful. No, she wasn't the hard-muscled, toned agent she'd been two years ago, outrunning him on their morning jogs or beating him game after game of handball. But she had a new strength. A well of endurance that drew him to her like a thirsty man.

"What do I do, Edward?" He heard the weariness in his voice.

"Do we agree that we have to get Nadia home?"

"Yes." Mickey looked up, and Edward wore his spy face, the one that made a man want to learn from him.

Edward nodded, a slow acceptance of their singular goal, and sighed. "I have a plan. One that involves an old friend and a trip into the past."

Maria watched Nadia as she paced in tiny circles outside the circle of filthy street lights. Obviously, the little spook was upset. So far, so good. Earlier, Maria had counted two contacts entering the safe house, two more leaving an hour later. Finally, a glimpse into the core of agents who made up Misha's net for information. The agent knew the plan would work; it was only a matter of time before Misha got desperate. Maria counted on the old spy's love for Nadia to reel in all the help he could get to send her packing.

Just maybe they wouldn't have to take her after all.

Why take her when they had the mother of all spies—Edward Neumann?

Maria watched as Nadia wiped her hand across her face, as if clearing tears. *Yes, cry, Nadezhda. Cry for Misha and all your empty tomorrows.*

CHAPTER FOURTEEN

Mickey had to admit he'd expected something more from Edward Neumann, master spy, king of covert, the supreme operator.

Mickey lifted the side of the blanket, where he huddled between two sacks of potatoes, and peered out into the drizzly, gray morning. If he could get any more miserable, he wasn't sure how. At least in gulag, he'd had Evgeny's tapping on the other side of the concrete to keep his hopes alive.

In this rickety, horse-drawn cart, the only hope around was curled up in a similarly miserable ball and not talking to him.

Well, she had said a few words, but they weren't the ones he wanted—*I love you, Mickey. I trust you, Mickey.*

No, he'd gotten the spy version of his wife. "What's the plan?"

She'd returned in the middle of their scheming, and from the look on her face, either the wind had whipped up and chapped her beautiful cheeks, or she'd been crying. Typical Nadia style, she hid it and, sitting down at the table, dove into the plans.

Edward had a map spread out on the table and traced the route with his finger. "The Velikaya River leads straight down to the Baltic Sea. It's an old trade route, and the monks at the Pechory Monastery use it every year as they pilgrimage to Ukraine and the monastery in Simferopol. I've hooked us up with an old friend who has agreed to meet us there and ferry you out through the Black Sea."

Nadia stared at the map long and hard. "Why don't we just go north, across Estonia, and out through the Baltic?"

Edward shot Mickey a pointed look, one that ran a chill up his spine. "Because I need time to clear Mickey's name. To prove this information is solid and to wipe the doubts from the CIA files."

Nadia's mouth made a silent, round O. She nodded. "So, how are we going to get to the monastery?"

"I'll take you over. I have a potato cart out back. You and Michael will hide inside, and once through the gates, Timofea will meet you and hide you somewhere on the grounds until the pilgrimage begins."

"Timofea?" She frowned, and Mickey recognized the gleam of curiosity in her eyes. "Seems I've heard you use that name before."

Edward folded up a map. "Yes. He was a. . .friend. During World War II. A brave man who saved. . ." He looked up at his daughter, and Mickey could have sworn the man turned two shades lighter. "He saved the life of someone I love very much."

Silence felt thick and prickly as the two stared at each other. "My mother?" Nadia asked softly.

Edward looked away, and Mickey's breath nearly hiccupped when he saw moisture in the spymaster's eyes. "No."

That one-word answer hung in the air a full minute before Edward pushed himself away from the table and into the next room. Nadia didn't follow him. She hung her head, and a deep sigh welled from her chest.

Mickey touched her ice-cold fists and squeezed. She didn't look at him as she, too, rose and walked into the next room. He'd found her ten minutes later, curled on the sofa, sleeping.

Or pretending to sleep. He suddenly wondered if her one-word, clipped answers this morning as they climbed into the potato cart had more to do with her father's secrets than her husband's supposed betrayals.

He curled into a ball, pulled his hat over his ears, and fought the early morning drizzle and gloom, jerking in rhythm to the horses' efforts.

Two hours later, he awoke to the sun boiling off the mist, the sound of bells, and warmth running through his body like hot syrup. He shifted and discovered that Nadia had moved over, huddled against his side, and her body heat had seeped through his soggy jacket, probably saving them both from hypothermia. Pulling down his blanket, he glimpsed blue sky stroked with wispy cirrus. Out of his peripheral vision, he made out the green and red and gold painted cupolas of a religious enclave.

"Nadia." He gently pushed a chunk of hair from her cheek, running his fingers through its softness. He would miss opportunities like this, seeing her tender side, the part about being married to her that he cherished the most.

His thought jolted him. Miss this? Didn't he promise Edward that he'd return Nadia home? He groaned, realizing her words had churned up the truth. Despite his declarations, even his desires to return home, he knew he couldn't. He would turn his back on her and dive back into his clandestine world. As if driven by. . .what?

Maybe this wasn't so much about being on God's mission as it was his own agenda. He realized, with a wince, that he was more like Edward than he had ever thought. *"That's what I said."* Mickey closed his eyes, feeling sick to his marrow. Obviously, Edward knew more about Mickey than he'd given the man credit for.

How could he surrender a life that gave him purpose and significance? How could he be less than he was created to be? He'd spent every second of the last fifteen years focused on being the best at his job. Making a difference, he hoped, in the outcome of the war between good and evil—his own particular application of the Matthew 28 commission. No, he wasn't spreading the gospel, but he felt like a gatekeeper of the truth every time he righted the balance of power.

Someday the Iron Curtain might just fall, and God's truth would stampede across the Siberian steppe. And the fact that he'd been one of the laborers who brought down the tyranny felt like a purpose greater than himself.

A purpose that still had him by the heart.

No, he wasn't going home. Not now. Not ever.

"Nadia," he repeated, his voice thick. He shook her slightly. She came awake slowly, her eyes opening, latching onto him. For a second, a smile tipped her lips. Then it died, and she peeked out of her blanket. In her wool hat, with her light brown hair sneaking out and the sun in her eyes, she looked delicious. He ached inside.

"Are we almost there?"

He sighed, snuggling her back against his chest, hating that he loved the feel of her close to him. "I hope so."

Nadia curled her fingers into her husband's shirt and felt raw with grief. He was leaving her. She knew it in her bones.

To the very core of her heart. She saw it in the way he hooded his expression. She felt it in the cold between them.

And she'd say good-bye without crying. Without begging. She'd spent a good hour or more staring at heaven as she roamed the darkened village streets, tears cold on her cheeks. In the end, she couldn't deny that letting Mickey go felt. . .right. She couldn't drag him home. Because, deep inside, she'd always wonder what desire boiled in his heart.

She wouldn't live with ghosts. Not anymore. She'd done that most of her life, dodging her father's phantoms, dodging the specter of her mother in her father's eyes. Ekaterina would not be a victim of her sorrow.

Nadia had deliberately moved close to Mickey, despite the warnings in her heart, longing for one last moment in his arms. Even if he held her only in his slumber, she could feel his strength, smell his rugged, die-hard essential Mickey smell, feel the hard plains of his chest rise and fall with his breath. Somehow, despite the agony of knowing that he was going to leave her, probably at the monastery, the quiet moment under the ratty wool blankets to the tune of the creak of the potato cart filled her weary bones with strength. She'd carry her man home in her heart and pour him out to their daughter. Not in grief, but in joy.

Ekaterina might not ever see her father, but her life wouldn't be bereft of his memory. Like Nadia's life had been of her mother's.

What had happened to Magda Neumann? Why didn't her father have even one picture of his beloved bride in the house? Why hadn't he set Nadia on his lap and woven her stories about the woman he still so obviously loved? As if her name scoured open a sucking chest wound, his eyes filled with a palpable pain every time Nadia asked.

She learned quickly not to linger long on the subject.

Especially after the night she'd found him sitting on the side of his bed at 2:00 a.m., the moonlight slinking through the islet curtains, splattering the floor. She'd had a nightmare, something that vanished the moment she heard the uneven breathing of suffering in the next room. Grandma's door was shut, but her father's stood cracked open, as if he'd been out in the hallway or even returned from one of his occasional midnight wanderings. The gust of a fall breeze through the unwinterized windowpanes in the clapboard farmhouse lifted her nightgown, and the floor froze her bare feet. But she inched forward, her eight-year-old eyes wide at her father's bowed, even shaking shoulders.

"Daddy?" she'd asked and been horrified to find tears in his eyes. He tried to smile, but it morphed into an unfamiliar expression. She touched his huge, muscular arm, the one that held her when she'd been bucked off Pumpkin, their roan. His face crumpled when she asked, "Did you have a nightmare?"

He shook his head, then, in a move that took her heart out of her chest, crushed her to him. Somehow, inside those solid arms, she always knew safety. Still, she felt him sigh, deep and long. "Nadezhda, I'm sorry. I failed you."

Nadia pushed away from him, her hands on his shoulders. "What, Daddy? What do you mean?"

He swallowed, and in the moonlight, she saw torture in his eyes. "I'm not a good father." He shook his head, and again his eyes filled. Fear ran through Nadia like a cold gust. He cupped her face in his hands. "What was your mother thinking?"

Nadia stared at him.

He touched her hair. She could still remember the way

his coarse fingers tangled into her curls. "I wanted so much more for you. I thought maybe. . .if I just kept searching." But he shook his head. "I can't find her, honey." He tucked her head into the well of his shoulder. "Maybe she is really gone."

"Who, Daddy?"

He closed his eyes, took a deep, pained breath. "I'll keep trying. I will." He kissed her forehead, forced a hard smile. "You're so much like her. Smart and brave and feisty." He ran a finger down her cheek. "I love you, Hope. More than you can imagine."

"I know, Daddy."

Nadia closed her eyes and wound her arm around Mickey's chest, her eyes full. She'd guessed, even then, that her father's tears had more to do with his broken heart than his failure at parenting. After all, didn't she have his wisdom, his courage? His passion for truth? But the things he'd named about her mother—her smarts, her feistiness. Were there other qualities Nadia shared with the woman she'd never known? Did her mother love the outdoors and running across the shaved cornfields in October?

Most of the time, however, Edward Neumann appeared sufficient for both roles. He loved her. Despite his anger over her marriage to Mickey. Despite the cold-lipped treatment over the past two years. Despite the fact he'd spent more time in another country, fighting an unseen war, than with her on the farm in New York.

The fact that he'd come to Russia to save her. . .that spoke volumes, didn't it?

She cast a glance at him in the driver's seat of the wagon. Dressed in a brown work jacket, his silver and black hair tousled by the wind under his stocking cap, he still had the wide-shouldered bearing of a man who knew how to handle himself.

She wondered, suddenly, how she'd convey Mickey's embrace to a daughter who'd never seen him. Acid pooled in her throat, and she blinked back tears.

"Mickey?"

"Mmm?"

She fought the tumult of panic. *Please, please come home! Please, write! Please don't forget me or our daughter!* "Remember that I love you."

She felt his hand under her chin, and he lifted her face to his. Pain radiated from his eyes. He tried a smile and failed. "You, too, Nadia." Then he kissed her, softly, achingly gently. She swallowed the pain welling in the back of her throat.

"Get down, you two," said Edward as he slapped the horses. They slunk under the blankets, hearing voices around them, then bells shrilling in the cold air, calling for morning prayer. The cart rolled to a stop, and Nadia held her breath, listening as her father spoke in peasant-accented Russian to someone, then with a jolt, continued over ruts and jars. She could feel Mickey's chest still beneath her hand as he, too, held his breath. The smell of dirty potatoes and the musty wool blanket reminded her that she looked like a vagabond on the run—hardly the last memory she wanted to give Mickey.

She closed her eyes against a wave of grief.

The cluck of chickens added to the morning sounds, then the soft *thwump* of a gate closing. She fought the desire to wiggle through the lumpy bags and survey their surroundings. Mickey must have felt her impatience, for he tightened his grip around her shoulders.

Or maybe, hopefully, he, too, felt the grief of their bleak future and wanted one last moment.

The cart rolled to a stop, followed by another soft *thwump* of doors. She heard groaning and realized they'd entered a barn. The crisp, tart smell of hay and straw and barn animals piqued her memories as she heard her father hop down from his perch. "*Drazvotyza,* Timofea. *Ochen Preatna.*"

She heard a greeting but couldn't place the voice. Not old but neither young.

Footsteps, then her father's voice closer. "Okay, Michael. You're safe."

Mickey tossed off their blankets, and a chill rushed under Nadia's coat. She pushed off Mickey's chest, feeling like something that lived under a log, and searched for her father. He stood in the shadows cast by the loose slats in the barn boards. Behind him, a jersey cow lay in repose on a bed of hay, tethered by her nose to the wall. A monk stood beside her father, large in stature but absent of menace. He wore a hood and a smile and the most curious soft brown eyes. Mickey pushed her up, and she crawled over the potatoes. She jumped down and braced her arm on the side of the buckboard. Mickey landed nimbly beside her.

Her gaze remained on the monk. He searched her, up and down, a light in his eyes that felt warm and made a lump rise in her throat.

"Do I know you?" she asked.

He smiled, and she could have sworn her father grimaced. Edward cupped a hand behind his neck, turned away, and, for a moment, Nadia returned to that moonlit bedroom and finally put a name to her father's expression. Fear.

"Oh, yes, Nadezhda. You know me." Timofea pushed

away his hood, revealing thinning brown hair. It added about ten years to his young face. She frowned at her father, who now turned back and studied her. One side of his face tweaked up in a chagrined smile.

"How? I've never been to Pechory."

He laughed, his eyes shining. "Oh yes you have, little one. You were born here."

CHAPTER FIFTEEN

They sat in the shadows and patterns of the sunlit *stolovaya,* where Brother Timofea was attempting to coax food into Nadia. Mickey noted that Nadia had the appearance of a shell-shocked Vietnam vet. Completely white. And that was an improvement over the pasty gray she'd turned after Brother Timofea's words. Mickey had instinctively reached out and grabbed her, realizing for the first time that Nadia had a true Achilles' heel. Her past.

Nadia had once told him that her mother had died in childbirth, but something roaming behind her eyes said she hadn't believed it. Until this moment, Mickey hadn't a clue why.

Mickey guessed Timofea's age at sixty-plus, although the way the monk moved around them with a slow grace, he wondered if the man hadn't simply aged well. He spoke with the wisdom of the ages as he fed them buckwheat kasha, brown bread, and fresh milk.

They sat at a long wooden table, polished by years, maybe centuries, under the elbows of the monks' robes. Sunlight gleamed off it from the high windows, but the heat didn't begin to fracture the chill embedded in the lath-and-plaster walls. A low fire flickered in the stone hearth at one end of the room, filling the air with the smell of smoke. An occasional pop and crackle punctuated Timofea's words as he outlined their escape. "We leave in two days for the Simferopol monastery. I've already talked to the Father. He knows Edward and has been instrumental in allowing him passage at times to the free world."

Mickey glanced at Edward, who sat beside his daughter. Furrows of concern lined his brow as he glanced at her. She'd said nothing since that moment in the barn when the monk had nearly flattened her with his softly spoken words.

"You were born here."

Which meant, of course, Nadia was Russian. Or at least half-Russian. Hence, perhaps, her name. Then why did she grow up in America? And did Edward also smuggle her mother out? Mickey searched the spymaster's face as he drank his tea and milk. Edward didn't look at him once.

"We'll travel by boat down the river," Timofea said in his low, smooth voice. Mickey wondered if he'd ever raised it. "We stop at villages along the way to offer services and blessings. Once we get to Simferopol, Edward will meet us and smuggle you out." He nodded to Edward, as if they were old friends in cahoots again.

"Nadia, because you are a woman, I'll need to secure you in the chapel in the cave out back. It is dry and quite comfortable. Misha, you stay with the brothers."

Mickey shot him a dark look. "Not on your life. She's my wife, and I'll watch over her, thank you very much."

For the first time, he saw color on Nadia's face. Pink, as if flushed and even embarrassed. He reached across the table and found her ice-white hand and squeezed.

"Nyet." Timofea turned to him, and anger washed his expression. It scraped the words clear out of Mickey's chest. "Edward will watch over her. You are a danger to them both."

Mickey glanced at Nadia, mouth open. Her expression

had darkened. "Brother Timofea, he's my husband—"

Timofea held up one thin finger. "And wanted by the KGB. If they find him, they'll find you. And according to your father, you're a mother. I'll not have you risk your life."

"Just what do you think I was doing when I came to Russia?"

"Being foolish."

Her mouth opened, but Edward held up a hand. "Stop. Timofea, Nadia is capable of making her own decisions. Perhaps if I had supported her and come looking for Michael, she wouldn't have felt compelled to risk her life."

Nadia shot him a look, one that Mickey couldn't read.

"But she's here now, and all I care about is getting her home safely." Edward curled his arm around her shoulders. "Stay in the caves. Mickey will stay with the brothers. And I'll make sure you're both safe. Just like I should have." He gave Mickey a sad look.

"Daddy, I can take care of myself."

"Of course you can. But maybe it's time I stepped in." He smiled, but the expression didn't touch his eyes. "Maybe it's time for me to keep my promises."

His words lingered in the air, weighted, as a look passed between him and Timofea. Nadia frowned. Timofea patted her on the arm. "Stay here and eat, child. I will bring your husband to our quarters and outfit him for what he needs to do next."

He turned and motioned to Mickey. Mickey couldn't dodge the feeling that he just might not be up for what the good monk had prepared for him.

Nadia stalked outside the tall wooden fence of the

monastery toward the cliff that rimmed the perimeters, anger pooling in every step. "And when did you plan on telling me I was born in Russia?"

She turned and faced Edward Neumann—the man on whom she'd built her foundation for understanding life—and felt as if her world might be crumbling.

He turned completely ashen and aged on the spot. She went weak as she watched him turn into a man who'd been burdened with secrets far too long. "I'm sorry, Nadia. I wanted to tell you." He put his head down and walked against the wind, toward the caves. It unnerved her that he seemed to know exactly where he was headed. She marched behind him in silence, fury fueling her steps. She was thirty years old. *Time to unleash the truth, Dad. I'm not a baby.*

She wondered, suddenly, how inaccurate that thought might be. Like an impetuous child, she'd run to Russia, needing Mickey like a security blanket. And now faced with losing him, she wanted to curl into a ball and hide. Maybe she feared being alone more than she realized.

"Lo, I am with you always, even unto the end of the world."

The words prickled her skin as pictures of Ekaterina flashed behind her eyes. Maybe it was time to stop leaning on Mickey and lean instead on the one who loved her like a child.

She had a feeling she would need all of God's divine strength holding her up for what her father had to say.

The wind picked at his hair and blew her own matted, disgraceful mop into a tangle. She longed for a bath or maybe just one of those cloaks.

"Where are we going?"

"Just. . .follow me. I promise, you won't be sorry." Did she detect a trace of resignation in his voice? She caught up to him, walking stiff-legged.

Overhead, the sky was a beautiful, crisp blue, the kind that hints of hope and sunshine. But the crisp fall wind mocked the illusion, scraping up leaves and whirling them around their heads. She followed her father into a small enclave, a whitewashed cave in the face of the cliffs. She walked past him, then turned, hands on her hips.

He cupped a hand behind his neck, as if squeezing out a tense muscle. "I thought it would be better to keep you from knowing. . . ." He shook his head. "Nadia. Your mother loved you so much. More than anything, she wanted a good life for you."

He came close, cupped her shoulders with his huge, wide hands. She'd always loved his hands, the way he could soothe her hurts, tame her fears. Now they felt weary, as if she might have to bear their weight. "I know I haven't been the father she wanted me to be for you, but I tried."

"What happened to her, Dad?" Her voice turned whisper thin.

"She. . .died giving birth to you, honey. Right here in this cave."

Nadia stared at the walls, turned in a circle. She saw where the remnants of a door had once been constructed over the entrance. The scars of the studs still remained. Inside, the rock floor was smooth, polished by years of footsteps. The walls smelled musty, rich with age, and perhaps sorrow. "She died right here?"

He drew a thick breath. "Well, not exactly."

She pushed away from him, searching his face. He frowned, and she could nearly trace time in his etched brow.

"I'm not sure where she died. I was just told that she did."

Like the flow of warm honey over her body, time

scrolled back. She saw years of frustration, heard his steps on the porch outside pacing. She remembered her grandmother's voice, *"Edward, when will you give this up?"*

"Never."

"That's why you returned to Russia. You were searching for her."

He swallowed, and she saw the truth in his expression. The raw, painful truth. And the unflickering torch he still carried. "You don't believe she died, do you?"

He closed his eyes, turned away from her, and shook his head. "Maybe not. I think I would feel it." He pressed his wide hand to his chest. "Right here. I'd know. The love we had burns inside me, and I somehow feel that Magda lives. Otherwise, I think I'd feel dead."

Nadia stared at him and felt tears pool in her eyes. "Daddy, that's all I ever wanted to know."

He turned, and she saw a lone tear trail down his strong face. "I should have told you. I should have never left you. I should have been a committed father."

She touched his arm. "You were trying to bring home my mother. That seems like a pretty great father-thing to do."

A smile broke his solemn expression. "Yeah. Maybe."

"Daddy." She licked her lips, her mouth suddenly dry. "Am I like her? Do I look like her? Was she beautiful and wise and strong?"

He ran his fingertips down her face. "Absolutely. She loved you more than life itself. I don't know how she gave you up. I suspect she died inside. But she was a wise mother, and she chose what was best, despite the agony."

Nadia's throat thickened when her father traced her face with his gaze as if seeing the woman he loved in her.

"She had a regal bearing about her and the endurance

to save a nation. I've never met a woman with more spunk." One side of his mouth tugged up. "Except you." He gave a wry chuckle. "Until now, I never realized how much you are like her. She was a hero. Helped save her country." He kissed Nadia on the forehead. "And brave. So brave it scared me a little."

"Mickey said that about me." Nadia wiped away a tear.

Edward's expression fell. "Michael loves you. I should have seen that."

"Yes." She steeled her voice. "However, well, he isn't returning to America with me." She held up her hand before her father could say the words forming in his expression. "And it's okay. I won't ask him to. He must choose freely. Or else he'll spend his life searching."

Edward stared at her, an odd expression in his eyes. "I'll stop searching if you ask me to, Nadia."

"No." She held up a finger. "Except, can you make me a promise?"

"Anything, *maya lapichka.*"

She took a deep breath. "Be Ekaterina's grandfather. I need you 100 percent there. And if anything ever happens to me, you step in, okay?"

He kissed her gently on her cheek. "You're going to be a great mother, just like she was."

Nadia wrapped her arms around his waist and leaned into his strength. "Get me home, Daddy. I have a daughter there who needs her mother."

CHAPTER SIXTEEN

Okay, very funny, Edward. Mickey paced the tiny, stone cell, wondering just how much his father-in-law had told the monk. Timofea led him to a solitary room equipped with nothing but a cot and a mattress. No pillow, not even a blanket to ward off the chill emanating from the cement walls. The situation had CIA termination written all over it. They were going to throw him away. Make him expendable.

"Timofea!" he called, furious when he heard the key turn in the lock. He slammed his open palm against the door. "Let me out!"

Nothing but the retreating sound of footsteps. He flopped down on the cot, sick in his gut. In prison. Again. Great. Edward hadn't believed him, and for all Mickey knew, they were going to shoot him at dusk and send him home in a box.

He crossed his hands over his chest and fought a chill. Groovy. After running across western Russia with the KGB nipping at his heels and the company spreading the net ahead of him, he'd been nabbed by an unarmed monk with a bowl of gruel. Some spy he'd turned out to be.

At least he wouldn't freeze to death.

Oh no, he'd be tortured.

Why had he trusted Edward? Mickey should have

known the man would double on him like a wolf playing with his prey. He supposed he deserved it. He had no doubts Edward could see through his skin to his heart and knew he had every intention of ditching the monks halfway down the river and high-tailing it back to Moscow—where he'd apprehend Lena before she could do any more damage to Aranoff or any of Mickey's other assets.

Then what? Mickey flung his arm over his eyes. Yeah, he'd have a full life then. After rejecting his wife in front of her father, he felt pretty sure Nadia wouldn't welcome him back with open arms. Even if she had given him permission to save the world.

Regret burned in the back of his throat. Nadia so didn't deserve this. The way she'd nudged up next to him in the potato cart pushed against him. She was so. . .unbelievable. Kind. Loving. Brave. And she was married to a man who couldn't be her hero.

Oh, God, what have I become? He turned onto his side and curled into a ball, choking with the weight of his decisions. *Lord, I wanted to do something right and good and eternal, but it seems all I've done is hurt my wife and somehow jeopardize the life of my best friend.* His words burned in his throat. *Help me be the man You want me to be.*

The lock turned in the wooden door. Mickey lifted his head to see Timofea outlining the frame. "Come. I've prepared you a bath."

It took two long seconds of silence before Mickey could push off the cot and follow the monk down the hall to a large chamber. A coal furnace at one end pumped out heat. Moisture clung to the walls, cultivating a moldy smell. A wooden bathtub with steam curling from the surface nearly made him weak with longing. "*Spaseeba,*" Mickey said.

"You're welcome." Timofea closed the chamber door and indicated a monk's robe and a coarse towel folded on a stool. "For your needs."

Mickey nodded, already starting to shed his coat. Timofea turned as if to leave, then stopped, his hand on the door handle. "Can I ask you a question?"

Mickey pulled off his jacket. "Yes."

"Why did you marry her if you had no intention of fulfilling your vows?"

Mickey froze, anger or perhaps the painful truth boiling in his gut. "I–I loved her."

"Hmm." Timofea's eyes brewed a troubled look. "I have found that we pursue what we love. I wonder just what it is you love?"

Mickey took a deep breath, suddenly fighting the insane urge to hit something. Perhaps a monk. "I love Nadia."

"Do you? Well, consider this, son. If you don't give any indication of your love, how will she know it?"

"I've shown her." He swallowed, not particularly wanting to discuss his love life with a man of the cloth.

Timofea tucked his hands into the sleeves of his robe. He raised his eyebrows, then, with a sigh, nodded. "Perhaps you'll indulge an old monk and allow me to share my thoughts."

Mickey glanced at the water, fought its enticing embrace.

"You were surprised when I told Nadia she was born here."

Oooh, family secrets. Maybe he didn't need a warm bath. "You could say that."

Timofea nodded, as if compiling this information. "Then perhaps Edward never told you of the sacred trust, either."

"Sacred trust?" Maybe he didn't need a bath at all. Mickey lowered himself to sit at the edge of the tub, crossed his arms over his chest.

Timofea nodded, then walked to the window, his back to Mickey. For an old guy, the monk seemed incredibly strong, unbowed. Or maybe they were all like that. Years of righteous living. Mickey felt about a billion years old with the weight of his sins.

"Yes. Nadia has Russian blood, and her family holds the key to a sacred treasure of the Motherland. Something that must be protected. Something that was stolen from the palace and needs to be returned when the time is right. It will restore faith to the Russian people."

"Stolen. Like a piece of jewelry?"

Timofea turned, a half smile on his bearded face. "Something of that nature." He walked to the coal stove, grabbed a poker, and opened the furnace. Jabbing into the coals to liven them, he then added another log. Fire curled gnarled fingers around the wood. He closed the door. "By marrying Nadia, you are now the protector of this sacred treasure." He replaced the poker, turned, and slapped cinders off his hands. "Perhaps you will consider this before you choose to leave her. And your daughter."

Mickey shook his head. "I don't want to leave them. But you, of all people, should understand the concept of a calling, a burden for truth." He shook his head. "When I was a kid, there was this guy in our grade, Lenny McMillian. He'd flunked about four grades, and by the time I hit fifth grade, he was the size of a grizzly and twice as mean. I was a pretty big kid, but he scared me. I think he knew my dad would never let him touch me, but he had his sights on my buddy Will. One day, he followed us home, caught us in the alley outside Will's house, and pummeled him."

He knew he'd captured Timofea's concern when the man frowned. Mickey held up his hand as if warding off the sympathy. His voice thickened.

"I ran away." He shook his head, seeing behind his eyes Will's bloodied nose, the broken glasses, his screams.

"My dad found me in the hayloft. I'd cried until my eyes were bloated and my stomach burned. He sat beside me and for a long time didn't speak. Finally, my dad, who by the way was a war hero, took the piece of hay out of his mouth he'd been chewing and said, "Proverbs 24:11–12. 'If thou forbear to deliver them that are drawn unto death, and those that are ready to be slain; If thou sayest, Behold, we knew it not; doth not he that pondereth the heart consider it? and he that keepeth thy soul, doth not he know it? and shall not he render to every man according to his works?' Basically, I took it to say that I was supposed to have stepped in for Will and anyone else who is in trouble. That God will hold me accountable if I know about it yet do nothing. I guess I took that to heart."

Mickey stared at the monk, seeing his father's hope, his passion in his eyes. "I knew right then that I was supposed to spend my life holding back evil. Rescuing those being led toward death." His throat tightened. "The thing is, I'm a Christian, or I try to be, and there is something about being a part of this purpose that seems. . .right. As if God is on my side. Despite the laws I've broken in this country or the ways I've deceived and stolen, I can't help thinking I'm on God's business. Sort of like the spies in the land of Jericho. Scouting out the walls, hoping they're going to fall. God led them to Rahab, and she hid them, and her actions helped saved Israel. That's how I feel about my job and my assets in Russia."

Timofea had turned back to the window.

Mickey studied his hands, seeing dirt in the creases, feeling somehow cleaner, despite the fact he hadn't yet bathed.

"I just want to finish the fight."

Timofea peered out the window mumbling.

"Excuse me?"

The mumbling stopped, Timofea turned, and a half smile broke through his stoic expression. "You are indeed who I have been praying for." He nodded, and his eyes bore the sparkle of delight. "I understand this calling, Misha. I am not without empathy. Perhaps, however, you will consider this. Once the spies did their job, they returned home. To their families. To their country." On the stove, another pot of water began to bubble. Timofea grabbed a towel and lifted it from the stove. He carried it over and poured it into the water. "I wonder, perhaps, if it isn't the calling that drives you, but your fear of inconsequence."

Mickey frowned, but the monk's words churned in his chest. "I'm not afraid of dying, if that's what you're asking."

Timofea carried the pot over to the stove. "No, not dying. You fear not living well. It is easy to die a hero, especially here. But living well a life that is pleasing to the Lord, even when glory isn't calling your name, now that takes true commitment."

Mickey stared at him, hearing Nadia. *"I don't want a national hero. I want you."*

Timofea filled the pot with water from a jug near the stove. "You remind me of a friend, gone so many years already." He sighed, as if expelling sorrow. "He, too, wanted glory and honor. He, too, was given a calling. And in the end, he was forced to trust the Lord to bring it to fruition. He, like the saints of Hebrews 11, went to his grave not realizing the glory to which he was called." Timofea set down the pot and walked close to Mickey, passion in his eyes. "I remember the day he and I sat together, in banya, the last time we were to be together, and he likened his life to John the Baptist. All seemed lost, and in the face of it, his faith stumbled. Just as the Baptist's did when he called out from prison, asking Christ if He truly was the Messiah. Jesus told him that blessed was he who kept the faith, despite the questions. Despite the difficulties. The glory had vanished for John. But he went to his death with honor."

"But he stayed to the task."

"When Jesus was baptized, it could be argued that John's job was finished. He was captured, and all focus centered on their true Messiah."

"Are you saying he died in vain?"

Timofea shook his head. "I'm saying that there comes a time when our burden is lifted. Our vision. . .refocused. Perhaps God is asking you to surrender one vision for another."

The steam from the bath had begun to draw moisture down Mickey's back. He shifted, then decided to pull off his shirt. His skin goose-fleshed despite the humidity. "I don't know, Brother. I think God would have to hit me between the eyes to have that happen."

"Perhaps He will."

Timofea stared at him, the hard look of doom in his eyes. Mickey gave a wry chuckle, hoping to ward it off. "Yeah, right. Let's hope not."

Timofea bowed his head, staring at the stone floor. "When a man walks by night, he stumbles. When he walks by day, his steps are sure." He lifted his gaze, pinned it to Mickey. "I suppose it would seem as night to a man if he walks with his eyes closed."

Mickey stared at him, his throat tight, his shirt wadded in his white fists as the monk shuffled out of the room.

Nadia felt as if she just might live. Maybe. She sank into the robe the monk had offered her, feeling clean, if not presentable. At least she didn't smell like old potatoes, dirt, and animal sweat.

Instead, she looked like a wrung-out street waif or maybe a hippie who'd raided the parish Dumpster. She pulled the robe around her as she stood in the center of the room, thankful Timofea had lit the candles in the tiny chapel enclave. Light flickered against the wall, writhing specters of shadow bending to the breeze. On the wall over a huge altar hung a crucifix—a likeness of Jesus on the cross. His hands bent in a portrayal of agony, but the artist had etched peace, even acceptance on His face. She wondered if she'd ever have that kind of confidence, the kind that came with completely trusting in God's wisdom, even in the face of darkness.

Nadia tucked her hands into the arms of the robe, feeling a chill despite her clean leggings and shirt. Unlike the other cave, this one smelled of incense, wax, and the faintest scent of leather. Behind the cross, etched into the wall, she made out tiny holes. Crossing the room, she skirted the candles, the cross, and touched the stone. Strange. Little shelves, and they looked like they'd been purposely created. She rubbed one of the worn pockets.

"They held altars."

She yanked her hand away and turned, her heart in her

throat. Timofea stood in the doorway, a bowl of soup and a hunk of bread on a tray. He set the dinner on a bench near the door. Leaves followed him in like mice. "The shelves in the stone. They held altars."

Nadia shuffled toward him, her stomach leading the way. "Altars?"

He nodded and handed her the bowl of soup. "Yes. Tokens of remembrance. Items surrendered that betrayed faith in a living God."

She made an impressed noise and held the soup bowl up. Borscht. Her stomach roared with greed. She leaned against the wall and ate, trying to dredge up her manners. "What kind of tokens?"

"Oh, books. Weapons. Candles. Crosses. This was once a place for travelers. They stopped in, gave thanks for safe passage, and sometimes left a marker of faith."

"I don't have anything to leave."

He smiled. "Not all markers are physical."

She drank the last spoonfuls of soup, then set down her spoon and mopped up the remains with the brown bread. "I came to Russia to find answers. It seems all I have is more questions."

He approached the cross, stared at it with his back to her. "Perhaps you seek wisdom more than answers."

She stared at him, midbite. "Yes, maybe. I'm. . .well, I'm a mother. And you must know I never had one. So I'm not particularly savvy on the mother thing. I sorta thought that wisdom would rush in when I gave birth."

He tucked his hands into his cloak sleeves. "A wise person isn't a person who has all the answers, but one who, when looking at the questions, applies God's truth, adds faith, and goes forward in courage."

She set down the bowl. "And what exactly is God's truth?"

He smiled. "Fearing God is a start. Understanding that His ways are not our ways."

"Yeah, well, I'm completely sure of that." She watched how the flame flickered across his eyes. He had a strong face, and it betrayed years of study as he contemplated her.

"His ways are those that are right and good. They express the character of God, which is love. This is God's wisdom."

"I don't think I have that kind of wisdom."

He walked toward her, put a hand on her shoulder. "My child. Why, again, did you come to Russia?"

She looked down at her attire, felt the fatigue in her bones from five days on the run. "To save my husband."

"For love, I guess. And why, exactly, are you returning home?"

She smiled. "For my daughter."

"Hmm. Again, love. It is God in us that allows us to love. I wonder, perhaps, if wisdom doesn't start with giving oneself to God and letting His love fill us. Everything else follows." He glanced at the cross. "I think you do have something to leave."

She frowned at him and saw a twinkle in his eyes.

He took her finished soup bowl, set it on the tray, and started out. "Perhaps, you would leave. . .Nadia."

The door closed behind him, but his words lingered, trickling into her soul. Her throat tightened. Nadia. She turned toward the cross and watched the flame flicker across the face of Jesus. Nadia. The spy. The woman who knew how to negotiate Russia around her pinky finger. A master game player.

As she stared at the bowed head, her eyes were drawn to the icon's hands. Gnarled. Etched with scars. *"Behold, I have graven thee upon the palms of my hands."* Again, Grandma's voice, but the words resonated in her soul.

Nadia lowered herself to her knees, feeling suddenly as if she couldn't breathe. Of course. She'd memorized the entire forty-ninth chapter of Isaiah with Grandmother. No wonder the words resonated inside her. They'd been a part of Hope for as long as she could remember.

A part of Hope, not Nadia.

Leave Nadia. She closed her eyes, hearing her heartbeat fill her ears, competing with the small voice inside. *Leave Nadia.*

Leave the quest for significance, the thrill of adventure, the fear of danger. Leave her identity. Leave her fears. She'd come to Russia to scrape up a life she'd thought lost and found it in her grip. But it felt heavy in her hands. Unwieldy. Leave Nadia, so she could return to Ekaterina.

"Can a woman forget her sucking child, that she should not have compassion on the son of her womb? Yea, they may forget, yet will I not forget thee."

Nadia's throat filled. No, God hadn't forgotten her. Had even seen fit to give her a glimpse of her mother. A glimpse into true love. Maybe, like her mother, Magda, she must die to her own needs and surrender them for her daughter.

Just as God had surrendered His Son for her. Because He *loved* her. And she could trust a God who loved her to help her walk in His ways. Wisdom started with giving her life to God 120 percent. It wasn't only about putting her faith in God and trusting Him to never leave her, but also about turning over her life to the one who loved her enough to save her from death.

"I have come so they might have life, and have it abundantly." The voice filled her mind, another memory of her grandmother, perhaps.

So, if she gave her life fully to God, He'd return it, in abundance?

The thought tangled her mind. However, she knew this. She'd come seeking wisdom to be a mother and discovered that the first step was commitment. Like her mother, Magda, Nadia would have to die to her own needs and surrender them for her daughter. Maybe a woman without a mother could find wisdom. Her route to being a good mother started with commitment. With love. With surrender.

"Lord," she said, now staring at the cross. "You've given me so much—a new chance, a new life. And I give You Nadia. Her identity. Her past. Her passions. I leave her here. Please, empower Hope to be the mother, the woman, You want her to be. Help me not to just be nourished by Your love, but to then live it out to Ekaterina and even to Mickey."

With a sudden rush of heat and joy, she realized that it had never been a mistake to marry Mickey. Because he'd given her Ekaterina. A baby whose name meant pure. Without scars. A baby swaddled in hope.

Warmth started at her toes, rushed through her, and filled her chest. It felt right and whole and pushed tears into her eyes. This is what she'd come to Russia to find, even ten years ago. Peace. Wholeness. Love.

She wiped her eyes as she stared at the cross. Love. That was the icon Jesus had on His face. God's love—the kind that portrayed the wisdom of God.

She felt emptied yet somehow lighter as she walked over

to the cot. Timofea had left a blanket, a burlap pillow. Lying down, she pulled the blanket up to her nose and wondered if Mickey had already snuck out of the monastery.

She couldn't swallow the taste of grief in the back of her throat. The poor guy looked completely unglued today when the monk dragged him away. As if trudging off to gulag or something. Wherever Timofea had put him, he wouldn't stay there long. *Oh Mickey, please be safe.*

She curled into a ball, pulled her hood down, and let her thoughts trace her daughter's face, the likeness to Mickey, and all the moments he'd miss. She didn't fight the tears. Let them drip across her nose, onto her hands. Just because she'd agreed to surrender him didn't mean she had to like it.

The door slammed open, a crash against the stone walls. Nadia jumped, sat up, her heart in her throat.

Mickey stood in the doorway, dressed in a monk's robe, his expression hard. His green eyes pinned to hers, screaming panic. "C'mon, we're leaving."

Nadia scrambled out of the blanket. "What? Why?"

He advanced, reaching for her. "The KGB. They've found us."

CHAPTER SEVENTEEN

"The KGB? Here?" Hope crossed the room in three strides and hooked Mickey's cloak in her fist, her gaze pinned to his eyes. The look in them seared fear through her like a branding iron. "How did they find us?"

He grabbed her arm, nearly pulling her out of the tiny cave chapel. Outside, the wind had turned mean and cold. It tore at her robe, snarled her hair. Hope shivered as warmth fled.

"I don't know," Mickey growled, looking past her toward the monastery. The barking of dogs raised the tiny hairs on the back of her neck. "Maybe your father's pal isn't as loyal as he appears—at least to the red, white, and blue." He grabbed her arm. "C'mon, we gotta make a run for it. To the river. Maybe we can ditch them."

"My bag." Hope whirled, ran inside, and scooped up her belongings. Her heartbeat raced her back outside.

Edward had joined the huddle. Dressed in the unassuming garb of fellow monk, he looked strung out and more than a little fierce as he whispered in strident tones to Mickey. "They're tearing the place apart, working their way through the monastery, and a few have already headed toward the river. You can't get out that way."

Flashlights punched at the night canopy from inside the walls of the monastery. The wind bit Hope's ears as it stole across the cemetery toward the little chapel, and she smelled her own panic.

"We have to hide," Hope said. "We can cut through the cemetery, and when they come up from the river, we'll run."

The look on Mickey's face stopped her cold. "What?"

"They're after me, Nadia. Yes, Lena knows you are here, but she doesn't want you. She's always been after me."

Nadia grabbed his robe and ground it into her fist, more to steady herself than to threaten. "No. Don't say it."

He wrapped his hands around her wrist and pulled away from her. "Go, Nadia."

"No, Mickey, I won't let you." Her voice shrilled, and she cut into a growl. "You can't surrender after everything we've done the last few days."

"I can if it will save your life." He grabbed her shoulders. Fire burned behind his beautiful eyes. "Three days ago, I didn't know I had a daughter or that you were a mother." He shook his head. "Three days ago, I was still a traitor. Now you have the microdots. You can go home with your head up—"

"I've never been ashamed of marrying you—"

"And Ekaterina will always be proud of her father."

"Because he died a martyr?"

Her words hissed against the wind. His eyes burned as he stared at her. "I'm not a martyr. I'm just trying to be a good husband. One who gives his life for his wife. Like I should have done two years ago when you asked me to go home."

"Well, I'm asking you now!"

His gaze turned steady, warm, and the tenor of his voice told her that her old Mickey, the one she loved, the one who emanated wisdom like a breeze, spoke. "No. This time the stakes are different. This time, I have to stay."

She blinked at him, fighting grief. Barking ripped through the night air. Shots fired made Mickey jump. His gaze darted past her. "Go. Run. No one can run like you can, Nadia. I'll distract them."

"Mickey—"

"Edward, help me." Mickey looked at her father, who stood inches away.

"C'mon, Hope. Let Mickey go." Edward's voice sounded pained, despite the steel in his eyes.

Panic rushed through her, wrung her throat. Let Mickey go? She gulped ragged breaths. She knew it had to happen, but not like this. *Please!*

Mickey set his jaw, gave her a hard look. "Don't forget I love you."

"Oh, Mickey," she grabbed for him, but her father had her by the waist, pulling her into the clasp of night toward the gravestones.

Mickey pulled the hood up over his head and faced the wind carrying the sounds of chaos.

"Daddy, no!" Nadia growled as she muscled out of her father's grip. "You can't let him do this." Still, she ran toward the cemetery. The monk's robe whipped around her knees, tangled her legs. She stepped on the hem and pitched, face first, into the dirt. It scrubbed a layer of skin off her palms. She bit back her frustration as she scrambled to her feet, her heart on fire. This was not right. She glanced back at Mickey, saw him turning toward the chapel as if heading inside for shelter. *Yes, Mickey. Pray.*

Her father's grip closed around her arm. "Hurry, Hope."

She gathered up the cursed robe and turned back toward the graveyard, to safety.

Light streaked across the field of lopsided stone. "Daddy, they're coming through the cemetery."

He stopped, and for a second she saw panic streaked across his face. "We'll go back to the chapel." He turned and ran toward the caves. "We'll hide. Behind the altar."

Nadia's lungs burned as she ran. The chapel door slammed against the wall as they entered, but Mickey didn't startle or break his kneeling-in-prayer pose. "Mickey!"

He turned, and for a second, she thought she saw hope streak through his eyes.

"They're in the field. There's no escape." Nadia grabbed him by the robe. "We're hiding behind the altar!"

Mickey's expression spoke mutiny. "This is a bad idea."

Her father slammed the door shut just as the candles bowed to the invading wind, snuffing them out. Only one remained, and light darted across the dirt floor and turned the cave a spooky orange.

"We're out of options, Michael." Edward led them around the massive altar at the foot of the cross and lifted the heavy velvet covering. "Hope, get inside."

Nadia felt Mickey's hands behind her, propelling her inside. She pulled up her knees and curled into a ball.

"Edward, you're next." Mickey grabbed the cloth and pointed.

Edward shook his head. "I'm too big."

"You're not. Get in."

"And what about you?"

"I'm going to pray."

Edward stared at him, and Nadia watched with horror as agreement passed between. "No!"

Edward climbed in beside her. "It'll be okay, *maya lapichka.*"

"Oh yeah? How? So they can beat Mickey to a pulp before my eyes? No, thank you. I'm not interested in watching him get killed. I'd rather make a run for it."

Shouts neared the chapel. "Too late," Mickey said and dropped the cloth. Darkness swathed them, and Nadia heard nothing but the sound of her heartbeat betraying them all. She felt her father's tension in his coiled breath. The shuffle of footsteps told her that Mickey had resumed his praying position before the altar. She had no doubt he meant every word of his petition, but she couldn't get past the scream in her heart to hear his words.

The door slammed against the grotto walls, and even Nadia felt the sudden gust of cold air invading the room.

"Kto dyes?" someone demanded, asking Mickey to identify himself. It didn't sound like any tone a monk would use.

She felt her father's hand on her arm. It tightened in silent warning. She clenched her jaw, willing quiet her pleas for mercy.

Without God's intervention, the KGB would have Mickey carted back to Lubyanka and put to the screws before dawn peaked over the Moscow cupolas.

Mickey bowed his head, stayed on his knees, and tried to stay silent, like a monk. However, his heart had leapt up and was already crashing through the barricade of thugs at the door, Hope in tow.

Why, oh why did she have to come back? He'd die before he saw her arrested. He fought to control his breathing, to center his thoughts.

"Kto, dyes?" the man demanded again. Mickey found

his feet. He kept his head bowed.

"Only a brother," he answered in his meekest voice. Still, his tone held the finest edge of challenge, and he immediately hated the guy inside him who couldn't stay down when whipped.

The man, dressed in head-to-toe black complete with leather jacket, black eyes, and a matching pistol in his grip, tore off Mickey's hood. Mickey didn't wince as the man screwed the weapon into his jaw. "A monk? Really?"

Mickey nodded, bowing slightly. He earned a cuff and fell hard onto the stone floor. *Please, Lord, not in front of Nadia.* This was the exact reason why he wanted her to run. Not only to save her, but to save her from hearing him die. Because he wasn't going to let them take him back to gulag. Not tonight. Not ever.

He tasted blood on his lip and pushed himself off the floor.

"Search the room."

"There is no one here," Mickey said softly against his thundering pulse. He pushed to his feet, feeling adrenaline build in his muscles. Maybe if he could reach the door—

A guard rounded the altar, pushed the unfriendly end of his AK-47 into the soft folds of velvet and, as Mickey groaned, dragged out his prisoner. Mickey's chest seized as Edward climbed out of his hiding place. He stood without fight and towered over the guard, who grabbed him by the arm.

Mickey wanted to hit something, hard. He gave Edward a pained look, but his father-in-law didn't meet his gaze. He stared down, resolute, defeated.

Not at all Edward.

Mickey felt ill. He'd summoned Edward here. If it weren't for Mickey's marriage to Nadia, she would never have run to Russia to save him, dragging her father along, unwilling, in her shadow. Mickey was to blame for the capture of America's premier spy. Inside he heard his spirit moan.

As Edward shuffled past him, he gave Mickey the smallest shake of his head.

Mickey nearly reeled. Yes, Mickey had delayed them, but Edward had just saved his daughter's life. They had their prey and a bonus to match. They didn't suspect that the real culprit, the real mastermind behind Mickey's jail-break, still huddled inside the chapel's altar. A guard grabbed Mickey by his tunic and dragged him out of the grotto and into the night.

No, this was not happening again. No.

"Run, Edward!" Mickey whirled and landed his fist in the soft flesh of his guard's diaphragm. A soft whoosh of air screamed pay dirt, and the man crumpled to his knees. Mickey would not be responsible for the torture and death of his wife's father—the only family she ever had—not to mention the man who had locked inside his genius brain every secret America had garnered about Russia over the past century. No.

He blocked a right hook by another guard, sending him over the backside of a dog. "Run!"

Edward had knuckled his way out of custody and now wrestled for control of an AK-47. Shots stripped the air, followed by shouts, barking. Mickey deflected another blow, kicked out his aggressor's knees, then hurdled himself toward another guard, clipping him across his windpipe.

"*Bwestra!*" Shouts from the gathering horde.

Mickey's pulse filled his mouth. "Run, Edward."

Edward's breath came out ragged as he rounded on Mickey. "No, you run." The look on his face rocked Mickey nearly still a second before a crack near the base of his ear sent him to his knees. His head spinning, he saw Edward lunge toward his assailant, but the cacophony of noises rang in Mickey's head, and he blinked away confusion.

A second later, he landed jaw first in the dirt. It tore off a mile of skin and scooped out his breath. Someone dug their knee—or was it the butt of their weapon—into his spine, and he writhed under the shooting pain. "Brave American," a voice hissed.

Not so brave, Mickey thought as the man handcuffed him and hauled him to his feet. Desperate.

Edward's expression matched his, bloodied and grim, as the KGB marched them across the graveyard and into the waiting black Marias.

Nadia huddled under the darkness of the altar shroud, feeling gutted from the inside. What had just happened? She held her breath, hearing the shouts, the dogs' barking, shots. She willed herself to dig deep into the resources of her training and find courage. *No, God, please.*

She'd died a million deaths when her father had pressed his hand over her mouth and climbed out of their hiding place. He'd flipped the cloth down, and she knew in her heart that this act was some sort of penance for the years he'd spent neglecting her.

Mickey's surrender also had penance written all over it. She clutched her knees to her chest and schooled her breathing.

If she hoped to get her heroes out of this mess, she'd have to make sure the KGB didn't find her. More shots. She flinched with each one. Mickey's lifeless face, whitened and bloodied, flashed before her eyes. She bit her lower lip to keep from crying out.

The voices distanced, became muffled. The dogs' howls became a mourning plea on the wind, their plaintive cry grinding into her writhing soul.

She listened to her heartbeat slush against her ears as silence ate the sounds of the posse. The blood flow had left her hands, and they burned as she pumped her fingers to kick-start the circulation. Still, she remained in her hiding place. She wouldn't put it past the KGB to leave behind a sentry to round up any lingering creepers.

The door banged open. She nearly jumped out of her frock. Her hands in a fist, she waited to kick out at her assailant. Her mouth dried.

"Nadezhda?"

The old monk. She closed her eyes and prayed for wisdom. Was he a spy? Had he turned them in, as Mickey accused? Or should she follow her gut and trust the guy, like her father? She heard shuffling as he approached the altar. "Nadezhda, they're gone, it's safe."

Yeah. Safe. Define that, please. As in, it's safe to go home, your heart shredded, knowing the two men you love are about to be murdered? There was nothing safe about failing the only people you cared about. She felt light years from safe.

She climbed out of her hiding spot and pounced to her feet. "You wanna explain to me how they found us?"

He didn't wince at the accusation in her voice but aged about ten years as he shook his head. "I don't know. Maybe one of the brothers discovered you were here."

"My father trusted you. He said we were safe here."

"I thought you were." Brother Timofea swallowed, and his eyes reddened. "At least you were spared."

"Hardly. They have my father and my husband. You don't seriously think I'm going to let them be tortured and executed, do you?" She stalked out from behind the altar, nearly shaking with fury or perhaps horror. "I need transportation to Moscow. Tonight."

"Nadia—"

"Don't." She tasted her frustration welling in the back of her throat as she tore off the robe. Under the disguise, she wore a pair of brown leggings and an oversized blue and white tunic. She dug out her bag from the altar and dragged on the grimy worker's clothing—disgusting pants, the smelly jacket. Oh joy, back to smelling like a ripe elephant. "I'm going after them."

"How?"

"Well, excuse me, but you forget that I was once a spy. I'll figure out a way."

"I thought you left Nadia at the altar." He wore a pained expression.

She hiccupped a breath. His words blindsided her. "Yeah, well, maybe I did," she ground out. "Maybe this woman isn't out to save her country. She just wants a chance to rescue the men she loves." She stared at him, as if daring him to contradict her, but the truth rebounded and hit her hard. She'd surrendered Nadia. Given over her spy identity. She was a mother who had a daughter who needed her, now more than ever. Her knees reacted first, gave out, and she landed hard on the floor. She shook and felt as if she might be sick all over the chapel floor.

A howl started in the pit of her stomach, and by the time it emerged, she'd tamed it to a low moan. "Oh, Brother Timofea, what should I do?"

The monk shuffled over, sat beside her. Said nothing.

"Ekaterina needs me."

He sighed and looked away from her.

"But how can I let Mickey and my father be tortured and killed?" She scrubbed her hands through her still wet, now cold, hair. "Don't I have a responsibility to them?"

He pursed his lips, then looked at the cross. "Rescue those being led away to death; hold back those staggering toward slaughter."

"What?"

He seemed poised to elaborate, his face drawing conclusions even as he stared at her. Then he shook his head. "There's only one choice, my child."

She peered at him, wanted to drag the answer out of his tired, slow brain.

"Pray for wisdom."

"Excuse me?"

He nodded, took her hands. "You told me you just wanted to know how to be a good mother. You know it starts with God's love. Letting it work through you. But God is also right and just. He is the champion of the defeated. He will know the answer."

Nadia gulped in his words. They salved the ragged edges of her heart.

"And whatever answer He gives, He will also then equip you for it. You're a woman of many skills, courage, and faith. If you let Him, God will take that and use it to work out His perfect will. His wisdom, His love for all generations."

Nadia swallowed the hard ball of fear lodged in her throat. "Pray?"

"Yes. God knows your needs. And your answer."

The silence of the chapel swelled in her mind as she tried to form coherent words from the emotions that knotted her chest. She was finding it difficult to breathe, let alone pray, and the most she could manage was to lift her gaze to the whitewashed cave ceiling. *Help, Lord.*

As if feeling her battle, the monk rose, walked over to a skinny orange candle, and lit it. A thin stream of smoke spiraled heavenward. Her faith was like that. Freshly rekindled, a thin spiral toward heaven. But fed, it just might point her in the right direction. *"Lo, I am with you always, even unto the end of the world."*

Her breath caught. That's right. God was with her. Only at the moment, she felt nothing but the roaring of panic in her heart. "Brother, do you believe God is with us, even when we don't sense it?"

The monk turned, a frown creasing his face. "Of course. God's promises are not dependent on our fickle emotions. They are fact. If He says He is with you, He is. Do you not know the promise made to your grandfather, nearly fifty years ago?"

Her grandfather? Nadia stared at the old man and shook her head. Brother Timofea frowned as he quoted: " 'For the LORD is good; his mercy is everlasting; and his truth endureth to all generations.' God's truth, His love, and His mercy are with the Klassen family, Nadia."

"Klassen? I've never heard that name before."

A shadow of pain creased Timofea's face. "No. Of course not. I'm sure your father is only trying to protect you. But trust this: God is with you. That fact does not waver, despite your fears and doubt. And that means when you ask, He will give you wisdom and answers to your questions."

He turned back to the candles, a bulwark of hope and wisdom as Nadia lifted her eyes to the whitewashed ceiling. She needed wisdom. But more than that, she needed God. And then God would give her everything she lacked. In fact, in *abundance.* Including wisdom.

Maybe it was okay to feel afraid of being alone if it directed her to the one who would never leave her. Maybe, in fact, God had used her desperation to save Mickey to show her the truth: that God, Himself, was with her, that she was never alone.

"Lord, thank You for Your promise. I do believe that You are with me."

Father Timofea knelt to pray as she continued.

"If I've learned one thing, it's that I might be able to live without Mickey. Maybe. But I know I can't live without You. Thank You for showing me that." She swallowed, building courage for her request. "Please. Please, please tell me what to do."

She held her breath in the silence, half-expecting to hear a voice, the great mightiness of God thundering in her ears. Instead, she heard only the soft swish of her heartbeat, racing. But something moved within her, the knots in her chest loosened, something wove through her, touching, healing. She drew in a deep breath and felt fingers of peace reaching for her soul.

God, please, give me wisdom. Leaning forward, she touched her forehead against the rock. Her watch, on the chain, fell out and clattered. The sound felt jagged and hot against the silence, and she jumped.

She picked it up. The metal chilled her hand. The little

black hands read past midnight, and she wondered how they'd kept ticking when she hadn't wound it.

"What is that?" Timofea rose and bent over her.

"It's a timepiece." She rubbed it with her thumb, memories like acid on her heart. "Mickey gave it to me on our honeymoon. It has a secret hiding place." She turned it over and clicked open the chamber.

Her heartbeat stopped cold at a white piece of paper, folded and shoved inside.

Her throat dried as she pulled it out. "How. . ."

She opened it and wanted to cry.

"Proverbs 31:10–12. I love you, my crazy Hope."

Oh, Mickey. "It's from the Bible. The priest read it at our wedding. It's about a wife of noble character. Mickey must have put it in there the night we spent at the circus." In fact, as memory scrolled back, she remembered quoting from Proverbs, along with the words, "Trust me." He had, and look where it had gotten him. She wanted to wail.

Timofea took the note, turned it over, then reached for the Bible sitting on the altar. The pages crackled as he opened it and read.

" 'Who can find a virtuous woman? For her price is far above rubies. The heart of her husband doth safely trust in her, so that he shall have no need of spoil. She will do him good and not evil all the days of her life.' "

"Good, not evil," he repeated softly.

"Her husband doth safely trust in her. . . ." Nadia's pulse quickened and ignited the adrenaline sparking in her veins.

Timofea met her gaze, and she recognized the truth in his blazing eyes. "I'll get you to Moscow."

His words reverberated through her and settled deep, fortifying.

"Commit to the Lord whatever you do, and your plans will succeed."

Timofea frowned at her. She grinned, feeling giddy, nearly buoyant as she found her feet. "Just something Mickey used to say before a mission."

"He's a wise man, your Mickey."

"Yes," she said. Mickey was wise. He centered her. He made her stop and breathe through her panic, her plans. Taught her more than he'd ever know.

But she was his Crazy Hope. And right now, that's what they all desperately needed.

CHAPTER EIGHTEEN

"All we want are your contacts. Who assisted you in your treachery against Mother Russia?"

Oh, sure. That's all. Mickey glared at the man out of his one good eye, pretty sure that he could still wrap the guy into a pretzel if the two thugs behind him would let him have a good whack at it. But no, every time he moved, they bashed him upside the head with a cosh that left a constant ring in the back of his skull. He tried to focus on the brute interrogator, tried desperately to not curl in a ball and let them finish him off.

Only, what was he waiting for? He already felt dead.

The dawn had the guts to creep over the high, grimy windows and into the cement room, where the bright fluorescence gobbled it with impunity. The bare cement walls gave no quarter, and he saw blood, not just his own, on the streaked block. The cold had long ago found his bones and begun to gnaw from the inside out.

Back in his underwear in the basement of Lubyanka. Well, freedom had been fun while it lasted.

No, more than fun. His last wish. God had been good in giving this spy a dying request.

As he'd huddled in the cold, vinyl backseat of the black Maria while they trundled him back to Moscow, his heartbeat had finally calmed to a regular thump, and he'd made out his own voice, in memory. "Please, give her a man whom she can trust, who is faithful, and who can love her the way she deserves. Give her a man who will protect and honor her and keep his promises." So maybe he wasn't exactly the model husband. But in the recesses of his soul, he felt peace. *Please, Nadia, go home. To Kat. Start over.*

Another brain-ringing blow across the back of his head thrust him back to reality. That, and the way Brutus fisted his hair and yanked his head back, washing the smell of garlic and dried herring across Mickey's face. "The old man is next. Would you prefer we kill him first? I know how you Americans are, dying for your countrymen. Are you sure you want him to go first?"

On the contrary. . .Mickey clenched his jaw, feeling crushed inside, and not simply from the couple of broken ribs. In fact, he'd do just about anything to save his wife's father. Anything—except give over the agents, sleepers, and moles that kept Russia from sweeping across America from sea to shining sea. He closed his eyes, fighting a thousand horrific images.

With a curse, Brutus hit his face with his closed fist. Misha hit the ground with a bone-jarring slap and just lay there, breathing. In. Out. In.

Another blow, this time across his back. Out.

A kick to his kidneys. In.

He cupped his arms over his head and felt two hands on his wrists, ripping them away. He thrashed, kicking at his accusers, and made purchase on soft flesh. They rolled him over, grabbed his hair, and slammed a knee into his back.

"Take him to his cell. Let him think about what will happen when we find the girl."

Mickey fought a silent scream as they dragged him

down the hall. Hope? They knew about Hope? Then why didn't they search for her in the chapel?

The bowels of Lubyanka gave off the same death aura they had two years ago. The smell of sickness and fear slithered down the moldy walls; ancient moaning filled the sounds of their footsteps as they passed by holes barely large enough for three men, let alone the six or ten that might be packed inside. Mickey prayed for merciful compatriots as they dropped him in front of a door, opened the bottom, and shoved him in.

Darkness, like ink, filled his eyes. Body odor and the stink of waste churned his gut. He rolled over and found his hands and knees. The rock floor drilled pain into his aching joints. He braced himself on the nearest wall and crawled toward it.

"Michael?" The voice was laced with the finest particles of pain.

"Edward." For some reason, just knowing he'd ended up in a cell with his still-alive father-in-law made his bruises less sharp. He took a deep breath. Pain skewered him.

"You okay?"

What, exactly, was okay? If Edward meant was he alive, the answer was. . .*barely*. Regretfully. If Edward meant the condition of his heart and soul, well, no. "Okay" didn't even begin to touch it.

"Yeah," he answered.

Edward grunted.

Silence felt cold and thick. Mickey listened to Edward breathe in and out, a rasping, labored breath, and he had his suspicions that Edward also nursed more than a few broken bones.

"What did you tell them?" Edward's voice lowered a

notch, just above a groan.

"Nothing."

Mickey imagined Edward chewing over Mickey's answer, weighing it for deceit.

"Me, either. I have a feeling it's going to be a long night."

"Yeah." Mickey gently probed his face, feeling for any broken bones. Other than his swollen nose, his puffy-*ouch*-eye, he felt intact. Well, at least his face felt intact. His rib cage felt in a million shards, not to mention his shredded heart.

Please God, give Nadia wisdom. Don't. Don't let her go for help. Please, send her home.

He wanted to howl, knowing that she had surrendered her father for him. "I'm sorry you're here, sir. I should have listened to you and kept my distance from Nadia."

Edward shifted; Mickey heard his bones crack. His eyes still hadn't adjusted in the pitch black. He couldn't make out even the shadows against the darkness. He pulled up his legs and fought the chill peeling off the mildewed walls.

"She loved you, Son. I doubt my words could have held her back." Mickey could imagine Edward shaking his head, his green eyes thick and full of pain. "I just wish I'd listened to her two years ago when you were first arrested and sent in a team to spring you. Forgive me for doubting your loyalty."

Mickey bit back a swell of shock. Edward, apologizing to him? "Do you think Nadia will go home?"

Mickey's skin prickled as their fears crept into the silence.

Then, "No."

Pain rushed through him, grabbing him by the throat.

"Yeah," he choked. "Probably not."

"Maybe she will, Michael." Edward's voice lifted, as if he was trying to dredge up hope. "She has the evidence. And she has Ekaterina."

Mickey grabbed onto his words. "Yeah. And I'll bet she's a great mom."

Silence.

"What?" Mickey asked.

"I just. . .well, I haven't seen her much since the baby was born."

"Why not?"

Edward moaned. "My pride. I was angry. I was. . .foolish. I wanted to show her that she couldn't defy me without a price."

Mickey closed his eyes as regret reverberated through Edward's voice. "I was the one who paid. Kat is a beautiful baby. Full of smiles and laughter. She reminds me of Nadia so much, it hurts." He paused, and Mickey heard longing in his voice. "She looks just like Nadia's mom."

Nadia's mom. The mysterious Magda. "She was Russian, wasn't she?"

"Yeah. A partisan. She. . .committed a crime against the Motherland. In the end, she became a hero. Probably one of the primary reasons Hitler's army failed to overtake Moscow." Edward gave a snort of disbelief, then groaned. "Sad thing was, she wasn't even trying. She just wanted to do her part against the Nazis."

"Nadia tells me you have a medal of honor at home," Mickey said, feeling suddenly that Nadia's stories of her father's past went deeper than she imagined.

"Yeah. But it is meaningless without the woman I love to share it with."

I don't want a national hero. I want you.

Mickey opened his eyes, feeling hollow and broken. "Yeah," he said, but his voice came out strangled.

Edward said nothing from his corner of the darkness.

Mickey touched his forehead to his knees. "I failed her, Edward. She just wanted me to come home. And I couldn't. I had to be a hero. I had to be someone special. A spy. A protector of truth." He shook his head. "And look where it's gotten me."

He closed his eyes, and they burned.

Edward gave a rueful chuckle. "Drop your nets."

Mickey looked up, wiped his eyes with the back of his hand. "What?"

"Nothing. Just. . .well, I remember a time when I wondered the same thing. It was in Berlin before the war, and one of my agents had been picked up by the Gestapo and executed. I knew I'd caused her death. For the next three years, I tried to atone for it.

"Finally, I just. . .gave up. And that's when Timofea told me something I just now remembered."

Mickey pressed a hand against his chest as he breathed out, wincing against the pain.

"A hero isn't someone who does great things but one who lets God do great things through him," Edward said with a tone that told Mickey he wrestled his own demons.

I think you fear inconsequence. Mickey leaned his head back against the cold cement as Timofea's words drilled into him. Yes, perhaps he did fear inconsequence. Didn't everyone? Didn't every man and woman want their life to matter, to make a mark on the landscape of time and lives?

"Seek ye first the kingdom of God, and all these things will be added unto you," Edward added softly, as if lost in time. "It means that if we have our eyes on the right place, we don't have to worry about who is providing for us or how our life will be used—God will make it matter."

God will make it matter. Mickey bit back the taste of regret, but it traveled down his throat, into his stomach, out into his cells, and settled in his bones. God may have given him a calling, but had he let God lead the way? Or had he run ahead, hoping God would keep up? He tightened his jaw, knowing the answer.

"The strange thing was, Michael, that when I started listening to God, that's when He gave me a reason for living. A sacred trust."

"And what was that?" Mickey's mind scrolled through the years Edward had spent training and protecting his agents, helping them gather information that protected lives on both sides of the ocean. Certainly, he could see how God had used him for great purposes.

"Nadezhda."

Hope. She was his reason for living? His sacred trust?

Yes. Hope was Mickey's sacred trust, also. A favor from the Lord. She had loved them both despite their mistakes. Their failures. Mickey closed his eyes and, embedded in blackness, listened to the ragged breathing of a man who might just be wrestling with the same despair. Silence turned cold as Mickey curled in a ball. *Please forgive me, Lord.*

His words died to a whimper as guards came and dragged Edward from the cell.

The rusty Zhiguli coughed and sputtered as it trudged into Moscow. Hope gripped the wheel and leaned into it, hoping that by sheer will she might eke the last sludge of juice out of the rattletrap Timofea had produced. Where did a monk get an old automobile?

Better not to think about it—or the idea that there was a lot more about the man than just a calm demeanor and a brown robe. Secrets were embedded deep within those coffee-colored eyes. Especially when he held her tight—as if facing the surrender of his only daughter—while they stood in the night-blackened barn, shortly after he'd coaxed the machine to life. Exhaust nearly choked her but not nearly as much as the look of grief in the old man's face. "I've prayed for thirty years to meet you. Your mother would be so proud if she knew."

As the dawn rose over the dingy one-room houses and cockeyed green-painted fences and glided down the rutted streets on the outskirts of Moscow, Hope suddenly realized why his words nagged at her like a festering wound.

Be.

Present tense.

Her mouth opened, and she nearly slammed her brakes and yanked the car around.

Not that it would have gotten her any farther in the old jalopy, but she would borrow a cow if she could unravel the meaning of that present-tense verb. Tears laced her eyes.

She must have skimmed right over those words, her brain fixed on Mickey and her present sorrows. Would be? The Russian Orthodox believed that the ones before them watched from heaven. Of course, her mother knew. . .unless she was still. . .on earth. . . . Hope's chest sizzled with new adrenaline. Did that mean her mother was still alive? She traced over the moment, the sorrow in his eyes. If he believed Magda looked down from heaven, why did he wear an expression of regret?

Maybe she should give more credence to her father's gut feelings.

Just like she should heed her own. Like, to whom did she go once she hit town? Aranoff? Or Lena? Who had betrayed them? She rolled both names around in her brain, feeling for peace. Lena was a swallow, which in CIA terms meant a woman who used any ploy to steal secrets. The KGB called it a honey trap. However, could that have been her legacy? A cover, just like Hope had played roles for so many years, from train conductor to cellist?

Still, Mickey was right. She hadn't seemed surprised to see them. And the woman had spotted her at *Belaya Nocha,* Hope felt sure of that. What if Lena set up the entire escape? But for what purpose?

She left that question dangling and tried out Aranoff's name. Sweet, protective Aranoff, who had purposely kept information from Mickey? Who had lied to her about Mickey's relationship with Lena, even her pregnancy?

Or had he?

She hadn't asked Mickey about Lena's so-called pregnancy, and jealousy wrapped claws around her heart. Still, Mickey was a man who, despite his deception in the public arena, had ethics at his core. He'd never been anything but a gentleman the entire time they dated, and he'd had plenty of chances, starting in the wardrobe in Pashov's office, to act on his male inclinations. No, deep in her gut and in her woman's heart, she believed Lena. She believed Mickey.

Hadn't she always told him that she trusted him most of all? Yes, Mickey was her handler, a spymaster, a man with knowledge and savvy flowing out of his ears. But he was also wise. He knew when to hold back, and she'd listened to him more than he realized. Like the time she saw him on the train and he'd practically threatened her not to try and wheedle her way into Colonel Lashtoff's compartment. Her heart climbed into her throat as she remembered Lashtoff's crudeness, the way he'd assumed favors from a train conductor that still made Hope blush. Thankfully, the guy was also three sheets to the wind, and before his advances came to blows, he'd passed out.

Just in time for her to rifle through his bag and find his list of suspected CIA assets. . .including Oleg Rustikoff.

Still, the memory had prickled her skin too many nights. She'd never told Mickey—but the fact that he'd tried to stop her resonated in a deep, cherished place in her heart.

Yeah, she could trust Mickey. Which meant he'd never treat Lena with the disrespect Aranoff had alluded to.

But didn't Aranoff say he loved her? Too many times to count. Especially the night of the Winter Ball. She'd been in his arms, locked in the gaze of his pale eyes while he suggested that they would make a great team, in and out of the company.

But she already loved Michael, she'd said, and hurt flashed across his face.

Yes, perhaps Aranoff had his reasons for not telling Mickey the truth, for weaving lies about Lena.

Did that mean he would betray his best friend? Or her?

The car coughed a final epitaph and died. Hope coasted to the ditch, shoved the gear into park, and climbed out. Her joints felt achy and tight as she stretched, then turned and snatched up her bag. According to her guesstimations, she'd have to take a bus to the nearest subway stop, somewhere on the Brown Line.

Hooking her backpack over her shoulder, she headed for the dawn, still mulling over the traitor in their midst.

The sun had climbed over the Kremlin and melted the early snow into pools along the cracks of Red Square by the time Hope surmounted the last steps from the subway catacombs. She stood in the square a moment, staring at the tomb of Lenin, and was again struck by the fruitlessness of worshiping a dead man. Father Lenin.

Father of death.

She shook her head and hiked down Okhotny Street, stood on the steps of Dyetski Mir, turned, and stared at the statue of Felix Dzerzhinsky, the founder of the notorious Cheka, the forerunner of the KGB. Behind him, KGB HQ, four stories high, leered over the street like doom itself. Dark. Foreboding. Hope felt dread wrap its tentacles around her. *Lord, help me be wise*, she pleaded as she turned and marched the ten blocks toward Lena's house.

An hour later, she paused only a moment, muscled her courage as she formed a fist, and knocked. Footsteps, then the door opened, and Lena's face turned ashen.

She looked past Hope, then nearly yanked her inside. Pressing a finger to her lips, she walked to her kitchen and cranked the radio. A Rachmaninoff piece, probably the same one that had been playing two days ago, rattled the windowpanes. Hope dropped her bag but kept her shoes on.

"What are you doing here?" Lena hissed in Hope's ear. Hope didn't miss how good Lena smelled in comparison to Hope's own earthy smell. She wore makeup, as if preparing to go out.

"They found us."

Lena's eyes widened, huge, panicked, and Hope searched them for deceit.

"They found the safe house?"

"I don't know. We were hiding—somewhere else."

"I know you were with Brother Timofea."

Hope felt as if she'd been slapped. An irrational anger clawed out of her chest, and suddenly, she had Lena pinned to the wall, her grimy hand around Lena's creamy neck. "How do you know him?"

Lena's eyes flashed, and she met Hope's grip with her own, slim and tight around Hope's throat. "Let me go," she rasped.

Hope felt her breath being crushed but refused to release the little traitor. "My father and Mickey are sitting in KGB HQ right now, maybe even dead. You tell me how you know Timofea and maybe I won't turn you in to every CIA operative in the city, just itching for payback."

Lena's voice rasped. "Hope, I am not a double. I swear. Brother Timofea is my great-uncle."

Hope measured her expression. Lena nodded, and for the first time, sorrow streaked into her eyes. "It's true. He's been helping us for decades. Even longer."

Hope loosened her hold. "You better not be lying to me."

Lena shook her head and wiggled out of Hope's grip. "No." She rubbed her neck as she stepped away into the hall. Her voice sounded tight, bruised. "No. It's true." When she turned to look at Hope, tears rimmed her eyes. "Is he okay?"

Something in her voice, the pleading or worry, tugged at Hope's trust. "Yeah."

Lena slumped into a chair in her living room. "I can't believe it. You were so close. How did they find you?"

Hope leaned against the wall, slid down into a squat, and lowered her head onto her knees. "I don't know. I just know that I have to figure out a way to save them." She lifted her head and stared at Lena. "And I need your he...

Lena looked up, her eyes red-rimmed and her lips thinned. "I have an idea. Something I've been saving for such a time as this."

CHAPTER NINETEEN

Mickey awoke to the sound of breathing, soft and light, as if not wanting to betray a presence, but enough to prickle Mickey's skin. He listened. The breathing stopped, and he wondered for a long moment if it was only the sound of his own panic.

"Edward?" he whispered.

Nothing. Mickey wanted to drive his fist into a wall. What if Edward was dead? How would Hope ever recover from the death of her husband *and* her father? *Oh, Lord, it would have been better if she'd never come to Russia.*

Mickey put a hand to his chest, pushing back the memories. Nadia, in her eggshell blue party dress, her golden eyes sparkling, Nadia catching him in her arms outside the Gorkilov Prison. Nadia, nestled in his embrace as they snuggled on the sofa in the circus dressing room. She'd barely moved as he tucked his note inside her locket. *Lord, let her find it when she returns to America and know that I loved her.*

You love what you pursue. He ground his teeth against Timofea's words. Mickey did love Nadia. But he had a job. A calling. And it would take a blow between the eyes for him to surrender it.

Almost without thinking, he touched his forehead and winced at a lump almost vertical down the center. *Very funny, God.*

ed the bump, memories burned into the around him. His escape into Nadia's arms, sy, but escape nonetheless. A sacred trust by Timofea. The spies of Jericho returning ho ecovery of the microdots. . .through Lena? Perhaps Go had been trying to get his attention all along.

Edward's words wove through the soft tissue of his heart: "Seek ye first the kingdom of God."

Seek God first. And all these things—a future, a home, a purpose—will be added unto you.

I will. The plea started as a peep, and his spirit screamed as he raised his eyes through the darkness to focus on heaven. *Forgive me for not seeking You first. For trying to make significance out of my own life instead of letting You have full reign. Please don't let me die doing it my way. Show me Yours.* He didn't realize until a hot tear filled his mouth that he'd begun speaking aloud. "I surrender my will for Yours, whatever that means in this dark place. I may not see tomorrow or Nadia, but Lord, help me end well. Help me to be Your kind of hero."

"*Zdrastvootya?*"

Mickey stilled. His thumping heartbeat had him by the throat. *No, please.*

"*Zdrastvootya?*" the voice repeated.

Mickey suddenly wanted to howl, or scream, or maybe just fight until someone could put him out of his misery. There *was* a presence in the room, someone flesh and blood, and recognition ripped Mickey open from the inside out.

"Misha, is it you?"

Mickey closed his eyes. "Yes. Aranoff. Unfortunately, yes."

Silence between them felt thick and hot and boiling a thousand failures.

"They found you," Aranoff said, pain in his voice. "I feared it. I promise I told them nothing."

Mickey winced, imagining Aranoff's battered face, fearing anything else they might have done to extract the truth. And if Aranoff hadn't given them away, who had?

It didn't take someone with a fully functioning brain to do the math. If Aranoff was in here, there was only one traitor standing. Lena.

Please God, give Nadia wisdom. Don't let her go for help. Please, send her home.

"Where did they find you?"

"Pskov," Mickey answered, his voice low. He hadn't the strength to do more than mumble.

"You stayed at the safe house in Pskov?"

Mickey nodded, then affirmed with a grunt.

"Did they find the agents there?"

"I don't know." Mickey pushed himself into a sitting position. Every muscle in his body screamed; every bone groaned with agony.

"Did you find Nadia?" Aranoff asked. "You didn't show up in the warehouse. I was worried. What happened?"

Mickey opened his mouth to explain. But how to tell him that Nadia hadn't trusted their oldest Russian friend? That she'd talked Mickey into running away to Pskov, to the safe house and death? He felt sick. He should have listened to his gut, even then.

"We saw the KGB."

Silence. He couldn't read Aranoff's steady breathing.

"I know."

His words smacked Mickey across the chest. "They

caught you," he guessed. "That's why you're here. Because you went to meet me."

He could imagine the fury in Aranoff's eyes when he retorted, "They don't have proof."

"Oh, Aranoff, I'm so sorry, man. I never wanted to involve you."

He heard a wry chuckle from the far side, through the darkness. Suddenly he wondered when Aranoff had arrived. Had he been sitting in darkness with Mickey and Edward? Passed out? Or had they thrown him in while Mickey slept?

"I made my choices. I knew the consequences." Aranoff's voice fell to a low whisper. "Do you know, did they get anyone else? Any of the sleepers?"

Mickey shook his head in the darkness, then realized Aranoff couldn't see him. "I don't know. I'm not sure who Edward called."

"Edward is here?"

Sorta. "Yeah."

"Of all the rotten luck. I'll bet they'll activate every agent on the side of Russia to rescue him."

"Yeah, maybe." Mickey ran his fingers through his hair. They tangled on matted blood. "I just hope Nadia doesn't go for help."

"Who would she trust?"

A name formed on his lips, and he bit it back. No, not Lena. Certainly Nadia would have listened to his warnings, his concerns. *"A prudent man concealeth knowledge: but the heart of fools proclaimeth foolishness."* The verse came to him like an old song from childhood. It raised gooseflesh.

Mickey paused, the old proverb churning in his head. Perhaps it was time to start listening to the words of wisdom instead of just spouting them off. Maybe this was the first part of seeking God. Obedience. "Maybe Gatsky or Romanich," Mickey answered quietly.

"I don't know them."

"No, you wouldn't. I try very hard to keep my contacts a secret."

"So, no one knows about me, then."

Mickey frowned. "Of course not."

"Except Lena, of course."

Mickey opened his mouth, closed it over a small groan. "Yes, except Lena."

"It can't be this easy." Hope tapped the picture in her hand, then tucked it back into the envelope containing the stack of snapshots. She glanced up at Lena. "Are you sure you want to do this?"

Lena sat across from her, looking like a scarecrow in her whitened face and red lips. Grief had her by the throat. "He deserves it. He's been playing me for years, counting on my love. Hoping I wouldn't betray him. I'm tired, Nadia. I'm tired of his games. Of keeping his secrets, of him treating me like I'm just good for one thing." She rested her face on the heels of her hands. "I'm tired of lying for him. After everything he's done, it's time he faced the penalty. Even if I loved him. He can't get away with this."

Hope set down the photograph and reached out to Lena, taking her hand in hers. "I'm sorry."

"No, I knew better. Mickey was always saying that a friendship with a deceitful man is a deadly snare, and I should have listened."

Hope's mouth tugged up. Yeah, Mickey said stuff like that all the time. A veritable walking proverb. Rough tears pushed up her throat. *No*. "Okay, if this is going to work, I need a shower, a new wig, and the best outfit you have in your arsenal. Let's see if an old dog is still up to his same tricks."

"*Nyet problema.*" Lena rose from the table. "We have to work fast if we hope to get you into place by tonight."

Four hours later, dusk spilled through the whitewashed birch and shaggy-armed pine as a KGB chauffeur drove down a dirt road that parted the forest surrounding *Dacha Sadba*. Hope stared out the window of the black sedan, watching the sun melt into the horizon, trying to gather her fear into a hard ball and shove it back into her stomach. Now was not the time to count the *what ifs*. Like, what if General Lashtoff had decided he suddenly didn't like call girls and was happily committed to his wife?

Okay, so maybe she felt a little better. She took a deep breath, feeling courage gather in her veins. She might have gotten Mickey into this mess, but Lord willing, she'd also get him out. She focused her eyes on a spot above the naked birch and beseeched heaven for mercy.

God's mercy felt overwhelming when she stared fully into her mistakes and her frailties and realized He still loved her. *Lord, I'm holding onto Your promise. Don't forsake me!*

Next to her, Lena looked like a million rubles in a sleeveless, white rayon party dress that showed just enough of her skinny legs to attract the attention of all the men in any room she might enter. They only needed one.

As for Hope, well, she felt like lumpy *kasha manaya* stuffed into sausage casing in Lena's black and fuchsia polyester minidress. When she stood before Lena's mirror, she'd longed for the misshapen and forgiving garb of animal handler, discovering that her dash across Russia, subsisting on black bread and jam, hadn't knocked off those ten-plus baby pounds.

Still, the added cleavage might help. If the dress didn't suffocate her first. Or if she didn't asphyxiate from the layers of starch Lena used to poof her black wig into a minibeehive. Thankfully, she still had the black boots, and she could admit that they, alone, added new vim and vigor to her spy bones. Even so, she looked like a call girl, and the comparison made her shift, as if wiggling out of the grimy caress of shady ethics. She never did like the deceitful missions. She much preferred the sneak-and-peeks.

If this one netted a very hungry and, hopefully, soused general with strings to Lubyanka—then she'd put on her game face and show them all that Hope Moore was back in stellar form.

Except for an extra roll around the middle.

She pulled in her stomach as they approached the dacha. General Lashtoff had only recently acquired the massive, two-story country home. Strung lights hanging from trees fought for significance against the twilight. The sight of three black sedans—KGB Marias—lined up before the arched entryway deepened the well of fear inside. She pushed against her stomach to calm a sudden tremor.

Lena reached across the backseat, wordlessly took her hand, and squeezed.

The sedan pulled up to the entrance, and two brown boys—conscripted soldiers—bounded down from their perch on the stairs and opened the sedan doors. Hope dredged up a smile and let them help her out of the car, suddenly thankful for the small arsenal she'd tucked into her boots and for Lena's handily glamorous wardrobe. They wouldn't think of searching her—not that she could hide anything in the sausage dress. She resisted the urge to wrestle her skirt an inch lower as she followed Lena inside.

Hope shrugged off the short mink jacket and handed it to the coat checker, then followed the raucous music pulsating from behind two white-painted oak doors.

Her heart stopped for a full minute as she stared at the ballroom.

KGB and party members, shoulder-to-shoulder, sporting brandy snifters and vodka shots; a string quartet pumping out Tchaikovsky; the smell of cigarettes and perfume; the sounds of laughter and loud boasting; dancers fighting for space; and in the center of it all, General Sergei Lashtoff, oversized, pungent, and already half-pickled.

Her prey.

Lena glanced at her, a smile tipping her lips. "*Oodacha teba.*"

Oh, Hope would need more than luck. *If this is God's will, He'll give you what you need to succeed.* She let Timofea's voice pump up her nerve as she hung her purse over her shoulder and sashayed her way toward the dance floor. She stopped at the edge, a smile on her lips, just outside Lashtoff's circle. Swaying to the music, she focused on her peripheral vision and watched the oaf gesturing, in the middle of a crude story, his dark eyes flashing. Her ears picked it up, and she fought to keep her smile affixed. *Yeah, you're a real hero, chubby, sending innocents to gulag.*

She remembered the information Lashtoff had picked up from Pashov's safe—files and pictures of agents connected with Oleg Rustikoff, an asset who had supplied information to the United States for a decade before being nabbed by the KGB. Thankfully, the film Mickey had shot had alerted the agents in jeopardy before the guillotine fell.

Still, the theft evidenced Lashtoff's personal vendetta—one that continued eight years after Oleg's arrest. Lashtoff seemed downright rabid to track down Oleg's coconspirators. . .and now she knew why.

Hope wrapped her arms around her waist and shrugged off the way-too-friendly advance of a squatty and soused colonel suggesting they escape the confines of the dance hall for a little fresh air. *Right idea, wrong rummy.* She shook her head, smiled, then glanced again at Lashtoff, as if sending a message.

Copy that. Colonel Squat moved away, flushed that he'd tried to make a move on Lashtoff's girl. And *bingo*, if it didn't stir the dog himself. General Lashtoff moved toward her, fire in his glazed eyes. Hope braced herself for the waft of vodka.

"Prevyet, Maya Doragaya," he slurred. Yep, same Lashtoff. She shook off the memory of his hand on her knee, meaty and way too possessive, or the spittle that formed on the sides of his mouth when he talked. Up close and offensive, he loomed over her by a good six inches of pure menace. The man had the power to walk her into the woods and leave her in an unmarked grave. Or make a call to Lubyanka prison and set free the two men she loved.

"Prevyet." Yeah, hello, you pig. She smiled through her clenched teeth, her skin already crawling. She tried to add a twinkle in her eye and only managed by dredging up memories of Mickey, his beautiful eyes watching her as she danced.

"You look familiar," Lashtoff said.

Hope ducked the spittle and shrugged. "I'm around. I'm a friend of Lena Chornova."

He raised his wispy eyebrows—had they been recently

singed in a fire? And what was that smell? Even Mickey, after two days on the lam, smelled better. She moved closer to the general, fighting her stomach. "This is your place?"

The general gestured wide, spilling his vodka onto the uniform of a nearby lieutenant, who stifled a glare. *"Da.* All for me." He leaned close. "Are you impressed?"

"Ochen." Very, very. She wiggled her nose. "I'm wondering if the general would show me around?" Suggestion laced her tone.

And he gobbled it like a wolf. *"Konyeshna."* He held out his elbow, and Hope hooked her arm through it. The crowd parted as they angled out of the ballroom. Hope looked for Lena, but her friend had vanished, hopefully with her own general on her arm and headed toward the staff quarters.

The tour ended, of course, in the upstairs chambers. A sitting room and, behind those twelve-foot-high oak doors, the boudoir. Hope dropped her purse into a velvet chair and stalked over to the windows. The night had engulfed the yard, blanketing the trees. Only light from the ballroom spilled out the backyard to the cold, stubby grass.

Hope tasted disgust as Lashtoff's hands settled on her shoulders. "A toast, perhaps, to my home? And its visitors?"

"Perhaps." Hope forced a giggle. Lashtoff turned away, stalked to his mini-bar.

Hope worked her 4.5 mm pistol from her boot and stole up behind him. "Not too much, General," she cooed. "I need to stay awake."

He poured, but his shoulders shook as if laughing. "No, *maya doragaya,* I think—"

Hope shoved the pistol against his neck. "Stop thinking, General, and listen." He stilled. "One twitch, and this thing goes off, so don't even blink." She fisted his collar. "Get on your stomach."

He swore at her and turned, aiming to cuff her hard. She ducked and landed her palm on the soft cartilage of his nose. Blood spurted across Lena's dress as he cupped his nose and fell to his knees. Hope shoved him hard onto the carpet and dug the gun into his neck. "Don't fight me. I have no problem killing you right here." Her own words, however, grabbed her around the neck, and she knew she was a liar. Somehow, in ten years of service, she'd managed not to take one life, a record that made her feel whole. *Lord, please keep him down!*

She dug one of the photographs from her boot and tossed it down beside his face. "Look at what I found."

The general stared at it, and she saw him age a couple decades.

"Yep, that's you. And what is that. . .cash? American dollars? And, oh, who is that you're with?"

She leaned close. "Now we know why you're so anxious to round up all Oleg's contacts, don't we? Hmm. I wonder. What secrets did he pay you for?"

"What do you want?" Lashtoff growled.

"Freedom. I want you to call your pals at Lubyanka and free Michael Moore and Edward Neumann."

Lashtoff gave a puff of disgust. "Never. You're a fool, little sparrow. You won't live through this night. Do you think I'm going to let you walk out of here with that?"

Hope shoved her knee into his back. "Oh, no. Of course not. But that's okay, because when I don't show up tomorrow morning at the Moscow airport, your own General Secretary Pashov is going to get a very good look at just who has been on his side. . .and *not*. . .for years."

Lashtoff's breathing thickened. "You're lying."

"Am I? Well, how about this? I have a friend with him right now, ready to deliver a gift if you don't call her within the next two minutes."

"I don't believe you."

"Yeah, sure. I'm lying. I'm also stupid." She leaned close. "You really think a stupid girl could bluff her way into Russia, into your dacha, and hold you down with a tube of lipstick?"

Lashtoff clenched his teeth. *"Ladna."*

At his growling assent, Hope backed off of him and stalked over to the telephone, her gun trained on his forehead. The sweet taste of victory swelled in her ears as she dialed and handed Lashtoff the receiver. He glared at her, his eyes now focused and very, very deadly, sending a chill clear through her and out the other side. She tightened her grip on her pistol, sending her own death-ray glare.

"No answer. It just rings." Lashtoff took the receiver from his ear and shook his head. "Sorry."

Fear lined her throat. "Keep listening," she said, but she heard her voice quake. Where was Lena? *Oh, please, Lord, help me not have judged poorly!* What if Mickey had been right and Lena was the traitor? She fought for control of her hand, her entire body, as the telephone continued to ring.

Lashtoff dropped it into the cradle. His voice turned sweet. "I'm sorry. The party doesn't answer." He took two steps toward Hope, and she saw a thousand evil pleasures ring his dark eyes.

Lena, where are you?

The door to the room slammed open, rebounded against the bar, and sent Hope jumping out of her skin.

She dove past Lashtoff's lunge and landed on her knees at the intruder's feet.

"Get up," Lena hissed. Hope's heart fell as she stared into a shiny American single-shot pistol.

CHAPTER TWENTY

Mickey burned from head to toe, his bones crushed, his head light and spinning, his teeth loose. This time they hadn't asked but one question before they began to punish him, and that one question lodged in the gravel of his brain. He hung onto it like a drowning man, over waves of pain.

Who are Gatsky and Romanich?

Mickey huddled into a ball on the stone floor of the cell and listened to the bells of triumph in his head. Aranoff had betrayed him.

There were no Gatsky and Romanich. He'd conjured those names from nothing and plopped them down like sacred offerings in front of Aranoff.

The man took the bait like the wolf he was and slunk off to his masters.

Gotcha!

No wonder they hadn't gone after Nadia at the chapel. They were planning to follow her to the nest of agents poised to spring Edward and him out of the clink.

However, if Nadia hadn't already hightailed it out of Russia, and instead turned to Lena like he suspected, maybe, just maybe, she might escape Russia alive. That one thought warmed him as he shivered into sweet, painless oblivion.

"Vsatvai!"

The command cut through the panes of slumber and jerked Mickey awake. *"Bwestra!"*

Mickey opened his eyes. Light dented his cell—a thin stream of terror cut away the secrets and panned across gaunt faces, terrified eyes. Mickey held up his hand as the light grazed his face. "You! American. Come."

His mouth dried as he worked his body into a crawling position and edged out of the cell. Every muscle screamed; his bones felt brittle and raw. *No, please. Not yet.* He still hadn't collected the remnants of his courage after the last interrogation.

A rough hand grabbed his hair and yanked him through the small opening into the hall. A hint of fresh air chilled the hallway dungeon, scraping the smell of mold and blood from the corridor and through Mickey's frozen body. He huddled against the wall, gulping in searing breaths.

Hopefully, this time would be the last. He fought his rising despair. How could a man wish for his death?

When he knew his job was over.

Mickey climbed to his feet. Yes, he'd unearthed the double agent. And somehow, he'd have to get that news out to his agents. But Nadia was wise. She would do the math, and he had no doubt Aranoff would be arrested and smuggled out of the country to justice before the month's end.

Crazy Hope. That's what he'd had. Their marriage seemed full of it, and even as he allowed himself to be muscled down the hallway, up the stairs, and toward the interrogation chamber, he clung to the memory of her beautiful, trusting, golden eyes. *Please, Lord, get her home safely.*

He could barely feel his feet along the cement pathway but kept up, even as they ascended yet another staircase.

The blue grays of early morning pressed against grubby windows on the ground floor.

He swallowed a choking lump. Execution at dawn. He hated the remorse that rushed through him. So maybe he wasn't quite ready to die. He closed his fists, painfully aware that he'd never met his daughter.

Raise her well, Hope.

The guard stopped him with a hand on his shoulder and shoved him against the wall. The cold jerked through him. "*Bwestra,*" the guard said as he shoved a bundle into Mickey's gut.

Clothing. A pair of wool pants and a knit pullover. Mickey stared at the guard. "*Bwestra,*" he repeated, and Mickey heard the urgency in his voice.

Why did they have to hurry? Did they have a pre-breakfast execution rule? He leaned against the wall and shoved on the pants, fumbled with the clasp, then pulled on the sweater. Shoes clattered at his feet, and he shoved them on, feeling as if he were dressing for a ceremonial burial.

Mr. Hurry-up-so-I-can-shoot-you grabbed Mickey's arm, and he yanked out of the grip. "*Otstan!*"

Hurry's eyes narrowed, and in them, despite the youth on his face, simmered fury. He shoved Mickey up against the wall, the gun in his trachea. "*Tiha!*"

Okay, so the guard wanted a *quiet* as well as a quick shooting. Mickey gritted his teeth, narrowing his eyes, not sure if he should attempt his last licks, when the guard handed him a stocking cap.

Mickey's heart fell. He put the cap on his head, and the guard yanked it down over his chin. Mickey tried not to taste despair as wool filled his mouth.

The guard turned him around, bound him, then

shoved him out the door. Mickey shivered despite his thundering, hot pulse. Winter had swept through Moscow with a vengeance, and the wind's sharp bite dove down his shirt and nipped at his ankles. *Let it be fast, Lord.*

He tried not to think about Hope as the guard led him, stumbling and tripping, across the yard. *Trust me, Mickey.* He let tears pool in his eyes. They ate into the wool. *Lord, if only I'd done it Your way from the first. Please, forgive me. Give Nadia a hope and a future. A new life with a man who loves her.*

The guard's grip tightened, and he jerked Mickey still. Mickey tensed, waiting for the shot, the burn, hoping it would be quick. His heartbeat snagged on the smell of exhaust, then the soft click of a car door. A hand on his head made him bow, and he fell into the stale interior of a state car.

He pulled his feet in as the door slammed, and with it, Mickey heard the resounding of his worst fears.

They weren't just going to kill him. They were going to do it outside Moscow in an unmarked grave.

He winced. His unclaimed body would haunt Nadia, just like the ghost of Edward's wife haunted him.

Rain, or perhaps sleet, splashed against the car. A gloomy morning for death. He heard breathing next to him and wondered if he shared the backseat with his killer. He fought the urge to lash out, kick, and fight and perhaps end up as a smear on the highway.

"Blessed is the man who does not fall away. . . ."

The Morse-code taps of his old cell mate, Evgeny, clattered in Mickey's memory. The message reverberated through his brain as sleet plinked the window. He listened to the code, let it resound in his heart. Yes. Even John the Baptist was executed. But it didn't mean he hadn't lived a purposeful life. The CIA would receive the microdots, and hopefully—*please, Lord*—lives would be spared.

Maybe he would die a hero.

He gulped in a deep breath and listened to his heartbeat as they wound through the city. The sparse morning traffic finally thinned to nothing, and Mickey guessed they'd passed the outer limits of the city. Still, they drove, the tires hiccupping as they hit seams in the pavement.

Then the spit of stones. Mickey tensed. A gravel road. The car slowed. Stopped. He heard a door open, then footsteps.

Mickey's door clicked open, and someone yanked him from the car. Mickey stood, frozen, as sleet pelted his shirt, his neck. He heard a whine, a high-pitched mechanical screaming in the background, and his skin goosefleshed. He balled his fist behind him, willing courage.

The car he'd just arrived in peeled away, spraying gravel. Mickey stood still, listening to the wind as it harassed the trees. Then, "Mickey!"

Nadia? "Nadia!"

Or was it only the trees screaming her name in his final moment?

A shot cracked, and his knees buckled. He landed hard, the gravel road digging through his trousers. But as he gulped in razor breaths, nothing burned, nothing felt broken. He swallowed his heart back into his chest.

"Mickey!" This time her voice was closer. And then hands on his hat, working it off.

He stared into the golden eyes of the woman he loved—or at least it sorta looked like his Hope, with long black hair and a bright pink, slightly bloodstained dress plastered to her body by the wind and rain. She looked pale and wrung out, but he could place that smile anywhere. *"Prevyet."*

He gaped at her. *"Prevyet?"*

She kissed him on the cheek, then stood and ran behind him. Edward stood, similarly bound, hat below his chin. Relief wrung Mickey weak as he watched Hope roll the hat off Edward's head, then throw her arms around him.

What. . . ?

He climbed to his feet, turned around. They were in a clasp of brush under the shadow of an outbuilding. Ten yards farther, on the rutted tarmac of the international airport, idled a shiny DC-10, diplomatic class.

"Prevyet, Misha."

Mickey turned, and his brain knotted at the sight of Lena, dressed to the nines, looking like her heart had been shattered into a million pieces. She had the business end of a shiny one-shot pistol—the same one he'd given her ten years ago—screwed into the neck of one very red, very angry General Lashtoff. *"Kak Dela?"* she asked, as if she'd just gone to the store for bread.

"I'm perfect, what do you think?" Mickey growled, but the saucy grin on Lena's face made him smile. "What are you doing here?"

"I'm defecting." She kept her smile, but he saw pain around her reddened eyes. She'd been crying. Confusion had him by the throat.

He glanced at Edward, who looked like he'd been recently used as a field grater. One eye bulged black, and he sported a bruise on his jaw that just might require X-rays. Preferably in Amsterdam or even in Home Sweet Home.

"Okay, you have your spies. Give me the combination," Lashtoff growled. He sat in his black Maria, one elbow outside the window.

Lena leaned close, whispered, and he gave her a look that might peel the skin off a dead rat. "Better hurry," she said softly.

Hope was untying Mickey's hands as Lashtoff roared off, disappearing in the gloomy embrace of predawn.

"How did you do this?" Mickey asked as his bonds gave way. He turned and, before Nadia could answer, grabbed her in his arms. She smelled pretty and clean and full of hope. Full of life. He gulped it in like a thirsty man as he held her close and buried his face in her neck.

She pushed away, her hands on his chest. He'd expected a victory smile, the kind she'd given him the day he'd fallen for her—cocky, full of fun, triumphant.

Tears glistened in her beautiful eyes. "This is goodbye, Mickey. I have to go home."

"Of course you do. We have a daughter at home waiting for us." Mickey cupped his hands around her face, soft, his thumbs caressing her cheeks. It sent regret through her like a fire, and she broke away. No, she would not spend her last moments with him crying. She swiped her tears, furious that now, after the horrific night, she would unravel.

She had to let Mickey go. She hadn't freed him to turn him into a guilt offering. She gulped back her fears, dredged up a smile, and turned back to Mickey, the man who lived to be a spy. "You don't understand. I'm going alone. You're not coming with me."

"What?" Oh, he looked brutal. A purple-black bruise around his eye, another on his jaw, and she was pretty sure those were fingerprints imprinted on his neck. She traced the outline of his good cheek with her hand, fearing that she might hurt him even now. But it couldn't be any worse than the pain searing her heart as she looked into his beautiful green eyes and shook her head.

"You have to stay here. Finish the job. Lena's not your traitor, we know that." She glanced at Lena, now huddled under Edward's arm. The sparrow looked like she might melt into a puddle, but she had the chutzpah of Attila the Hun, the way she'd scared Lashtoff into obedience.

"Get up!" Lena's voice briefly slashed through Hope's memory. That, and the way Lena had turned the weapon on Lashtoff. "Get off that floor and listen good." Silhouetted by the door, she'd looked ethereal in her white dress, her shapely legs in a pair of high pumps. She practically glimmered. Or maybe it was the look of triumph on her face, as if she'd beaten her greatest enemy.

"I just left General Secretary Pashov in a stupor in his limousine. He's headed home to sleep it off. And I suppose in the morning, he'll start wondering where his keys are." She held them up, dangled them like bait. "But of course, you'll have them. Which is a good thing, because you'll need them to get into his office."

Lashtoff made a lunge for them, but Lena jerked them away. The low, carefully etched fury in her voice was enough to make Lashtoff stop and stare at her. Fear mingled with the anger in his eyes, and suddenly, Hope realized why Lena had left her post.

She knew Hope needed her help.

So maybe Hope had chosen wisely when she followed her heart and trusted Lena instead of Aranoff.

Thank You, God. He hadn't forsaken her. And one choice at a time would give her the wisdom she needed to be the spy, the wife, the mother she longed to be. *"If you let Him, God will take that and use it to work out His perfect will. His wisdom, His love for all generations."* Her throat tightened as she found her pistol and centered it on Lashtoff.

"What makes you think I won't kill you both now and take the keys?" Lashtoff had snorted.

Lena affected a pose that Hope recognized from *Zhenshina Belaya Nocha,* pure sparrow, sweet and sinister. "Because the pictures, all twelve of them, are beautiful shots of you and Oleg and my cousin. Unfortunately, he didn't realize that I've been following him for years. Anyway, they're all in Pashov's safe. And when we get to the airport, along with Edward and Michael, I'll tell you the combination." She shook the keys. "Better move fast. I don't know how long he'll be out before he realizes he's alone."

Her voice strained on the last word, and Hope couldn't help wondering what sacrifices Lena had made during the course of the evening.

"Hope, I'm not staying." Mickey's voice, his gaze in hers, yanked her through the still-simmering panic that he would end up in an unmarked grave in the middle of Siberia. He cupped her face. "I know who the traitor is. It's Aranoff."

"Are you sure?"

Mickey's expression voiced his grief. "I am. Even if we don't find him, his days as a spy are over." Mickey leaned close, his lips brushing hers. "As are mine." His voice roughened. "I'm just sorry it took God knocking me upside the head more than once to get my attention."

Hope felt a smile building in her chest, but she shook her head, fighting it back. "Don't come home on account of me or Kat. You have to choose this—" she placed her hand on his chest "—in here. You have to know it's right."

The wind tousled his grimy hair and sent a smell back to her that, without the padding of a fresh breeze, just might drop her to her knees. But his smile couldn't have been more refreshing, sweet. "It's right. I know it. I've completed my mission here, and I'm headed home." His gaze traveled over her face, as if drinking her in. "I have you—my Crazy Hope—to confirm that this is just what God wants."

Then he kissed her. So sweet, so impossibly tender, she felt her heart rise up right outside her body and dance. She leaned into his embrace, feeling his arms go around her, holding tight, holding her. Holding their future.

" 'Who can find a virtuous woman? for her price is far above rubies,' " Mickey murmured into her ear just before they turned and ran over the slick tarmac to the waiting plane. " 'The heart of her husband doth safely trust in her, and she will do him good and not evil all the days of her life.' "

Hope glanced at her father, his dark hair parted by the rain, his eyes fierce, and she heard again Timofea's words: *"Your mother would be so proud if she knew."*

Tears clogged her throat. *Sorry, Dad.*

Still, she had the souvenir from Russia—a legacy of sacrifice, of courage, of wisdom, and of faith.

A legacy she just might pass on to her daughter.

Mission accomplished.

EPILOGUE

If it weren't for the sunlight striping the room, glazing her eyes with hues of gold and pink, Hope might have slept until the next millennium, or at least until Ekaterina trundled out of her toddler bed and smacked her pudgy hands against her mother's face.

Ekaterina.

Hope sat bolt upright, the covers falling to her waist. Cold air licked the bedroom, raising gooseflesh. She held her breath, listening for her daughter's cries, snuffs of discontentment from the next room. The one-hundred-year-old farmhouse had little in the way of soundproofing, despite its character and cozy squeaks.

Laughter. Giggles. The sound of a toddler squealing reached out and squeezed her heart. Probably Grandmother had heard Ekaterina's stirrings and gotten her up early.

Hope flipped back the covers, slid out of bed, and pulled on a robe. Padding down the hall, she peeked into Ekaterina's bedroom, expecting to see Grandmother rocking Ekaterina or playing patty-cake.

No.

Idiotic tears filled her eyes. Mickey lay on his back, clad only in his sweatpants, his daughter straddling his chest as he tickled her. Ekaterina launched back in laughter. He caught her in his strong arms and tickled her again before cradling her to his chest and burying his face in her downy hair.

The look of love on his face made Hope sink to the floor, one hand on the doorframe.

He startled, looked at her, and a half smile creased his face. "Good morning."

"Hiya," Hope replied, but it sounded more like a croak.

"She was awake." He looked slightly guilty as he said it, and Hope realized he still didn't feel comfortable in the father role, rushing to Ekaterina's needs instinctively, knowing she was also his to care for. But he'd only been back a few days. After analyzing the microdots Mickey had hidden in the postcards, the CIA declared him innocent of treason. They'd wrung Mickey dry of answers to their questions and sent him home.

Home.

Where they might live permanently, Hope still didn't know. Mickey hinted at a position as a trainer or perhaps a handler, but for now, perhaps always in a way, home would be the farm in Schenectady.

Home. Mickey was home.

The realization thickened her throat. She crawled across the wooden floor, sat next to him on the throw rug. He looked downright delectable lying there, his muscles wrapped around their daughter. Hope stamped down a sudden urge to put Ekaterina back into her crib and entice Mickey back into the other room. The thought put a smile on her face.

"Have I ever told you how beautiful you are?" Mickey reached out, touched her cheek with soft fingers.

Hope felt a blush warm her cheeks. "Yes. Last night, I think."

Mischief gleamed in his eyes. "Oh, yeah," he said.

She shook her head in mock disapproval and reached out for Ekaterina. "Playtime is over. We need to help Grandma get ready for Thanksgiving." She put her daughter over her shoulder and laid her on the dressing table. "Lena will be here soon."

Although Lena had months left of her debriefings at Langley, the powers that be had let the former KGB sparrow take a leave to join her friends for her first American holiday. Edward had driven down to Washington last night to pick her up.

Hope startled as Mickey wound his arms around her waist, pulled her to his chest. He smelled fresh and strong, and she fit well in the pocket of his embrace. The feeling was enough to make a girl's knees buckle, just so he'd swoop her into his arms. "I'm thinking that Ekaterina looks tired," he murmured. "And Lena won't be here for a while, right?" He kissed her neck, and warmth ran in a rush down to her toes.

"Mickey."

"Mmm?" He cupped her face, turned it, and kissed her. She felt herself melting into his embrace. Loving this man took no effort at all. Especially this Mickey, who had healed and begun to fill out in mass as well as confidence. He was larger than life, her voice of reason, and the love of her life.

God had been more than merciful in bringing Mickey home. He'd given them a new start. A new foundation on which to build. No more lies. No more Crazy Hope. God had not forsaken the woman who trusted Him. And He'd give her the wisdom to teach Ekaterina the meaning of faith. One day at a time, for this generation and the next.

"*'For the* LORD *is good; his mercy is everlasting; and his truth endureth to all generations.'* " Old Timofea's voice filled her mind as Mickey stepped away and leaned against the doorjamb, his arms crossed over his bare chest.

"Did your dad mention anything about Aranoff when he left? I was hoping they found him." It hadn't been difficult to splice together Aranoff's plan once Lena, Mickey, and Hope intertwined the threads of his duplicity. KGB Colonel Aranoff Chornov, aka the infamous Maria—who had been a file-thick rumor circulating Langley for years—had been working against the CIA for over a decade.

Killing agents, twisting secrets for the Motherland.

Mickey believed Aranoff's love for Hope had been genuine, however, and the moment she fled the country due to Aranoff's conniving, he had turned his sights on Mickey. When torture hadn't produced the names of assets living in the Soviet Union, Aranoff had masterminded game plan B to lure Hope back into the country. He'd hoped to use Mickey's love for her and desperation to save her to draw the CIA assets out of hiding. The capture of Edward Neumann and Mickey Moore would have been Aranoff's greatest coup. His plan may have worked if God hadn't been on their side.

"No," she answered Mickey. "No one has seen him."

Mickey pursed his lips, looked down at the floor. Hope saw his hands tighten on his arms, turning white, and she wondered what unfinished business he contemplated. Fear tightened her chest.

She had no doubt if either Mickey or Edward stepped foot in Russia again, they'd be hunted down, tortured, and executed.

A shiver rattled through her. *I'm sorry, Dad.* She still hadn't summoned the courage to ask her father about Timofea's cryptic words in the chapel regarding the promise made to the Klassen family. Or betray that her mother might still be alive. He'd be on the next plane to Russia before Hope could blink.

If her mother was still alive, why had Edward left her in Russia? And what was the promise God had made to Hope's grandfather and why? The questions ringed Hope's mind like a soft, persistent throb.

Perhaps some secrets were better left buried—at least until their family's reputation behind the Iron Curtain died to a cold ember. Someday, she would ask questions. . . and maybe find answers.

"Hope, honey, are you okay?" Mickey was frowning at her, and she forced a smile.

"Yes. Just thinking how I'm looking forward to some Thanksgiving turkey."

He narrowed his eyes but said nothing as she finished changing Ekaterina. Her daughter yawned, and Hope couldn't help but kiss her soft cheek as she drew her into her arms.

Ekaterina curled into a ball, ready for her early morning nap as Hope settled her back in the crib. "You wore her out," she said as she tucked the blanket over her.

"I have that effect on the women in my life." He took Hope's hand and pulled her out of Ekaterina's room, a smile on his face that told her that Thanksgiving dinner was the last thing on his mind.

She laughed. "Oh, Mickey. You're such a troublemaker."

"You know it, baby." He pulled her into their room, into his embrace, and toed the door shut.

And anyone looking at her would see a woman lost in her husband's love, dancing to the music of God's grace, living a life of honesty and faith.

A life of Hope.

Susan K. Downs

Susan served as the Russian adoption program coordinator for one of America's oldest adoption agencies prior to her decision to leave the social work field and devote herself full-time to writing and editing fiction. Through her adoption work, however, she developed a love for all things Russian and an unquenchable curiosity of Russian history and culture.

A series of miraculous events led Susan and her minister-husband to adopt from Korea two of their five children. The adoptions of their daughters precipitated a five-year mission assignment in South Korea, which, in turn, paved the way for Susan's work in international adoption and her Russian experiences. The Downses currently reside in Canton, Ohio. Read more about Susan's writing/editing ministry and her family at www.susankdowns.com.

Susan May Warren

Susan May Warren and her family recently returned home after working for eight years in Khabarovsk, far east Russia. Deeply influenced and blessed by the faith of the Russian Christians, she longed to write a story that revealed their faith during their dark years of persecution and a story of their impact on today's generation. *The Heirs of Anton* is the fruition of these hopes. Now writing full-time in northern Minnesota while her husband, Andrew, manages a lodge, Susan is the author of both novels and novellas. She draws upon her rich experience on both sides of the ocean to write stories that stir the Christian soul. Find out more about Susan and her writing at www.susanmaywarren.com.

If you enjoyed the

family saga

NADIA

then read:

EKATERINA

By Susan K. Downs and Susan May Warren

ISBN 1-59310-161-9

Wherever Christian books are sold

Don't miss the next book in the

family saga.

MARINA

By Susan K. Downs and Susan May Warren

ISBN 1-59310-350-6

COMING MARCH 2005

Wherever Christian books are sold

PROLOGUE

PSKOV, RUSSIA
1941

In the quietest, most fragile corner of her heart, Marina knew Dmitri would abandon her—just as her parents had.

Marina Antonovna Klassen Vasileva barely restrained herself from crumpling at her husband's feet as she watched him pack his meager belongings: a comb, his Bible—pieces of his life snatched from hers, leaving gaping, ragged holes in her chest.

It was quite possible she'd never be whole again.

"I can't believe you volunteered." Her voice sounded ghostly, to match her dying spirit. Marina sat at the end of the wooden bed, her knees pulled up to her chest so as to hold in her heart lest it shatter. Her gaze fell away from her new husband, from his movements at the mirror as he adjusted his olive green Russian army uniform. She couldn't bear the expression of anticipation on his face.

"It's not too soon." Dmitri turned, and Marina couldn't ignore the way her pulse notched up a beat when his sweet, honey brown eyes traveled over her. He always had the ability to reduce her to a puddle of kasha with a smile, and now, the sadness on his face stirred away her fury. She bit her trembling lip and blinked back tears, feeling only weak. He took a step toward her and ran his strong hand over her hair. "The Motherland needs me. Hitler can't be trusted, and our Fearless Leader needs us to guard our new lands."

Marina knew more than loyalty beat in his wide, muscled chest. Dmitri longed to see the world. Taste adventure. She could hardly blame her peasant husband for his enthusiasm. He'd been offered a chance to explore the new land Stalin had annexed for Russia—Lvov, Ukraine. The world outside of Pskov suddenly called to him in volumes he, at twenty, couldn't begin to ignore.

Didn't he hear his bride, their future calling him as well? Marina pressed her fingertips into her eyes. "Promise me you'll come back."

His shiny new leather boots—the first pair of new shoes he'd ever owned—squeaked as he knelt beside her. "Of course, *maya dorogaya*. Russia is not fighting a war. We're simply reminding the fascist Nazis that we're here on the other side of the border and that they need to stay in their yard. I'll be back before the potato harvest."

Marina opened her eyes, attempting a smile at his humor. She ran a trembling finger along his square jaw, taking in every last detail—the way his dark hair curled around his ears, the scar on his chin from a childhood brawl, the rapscallion curve of his smile. Her chest constricted, and she fought for breath, nearly drowning beneath a cascading sense of loss.

"Oh, Marina," Dmitri said, and the texture of his voice caused tears to flow down her cheeks. He pulled her to his chest. Her cheek rubbed against rough wool, and the smell of mothballs obliterated his masculine, earthy farmer's scent.

"You're all I have," she whispered.

He leaned away and cupped her face between his hands. His eyes darkened. "That's not true."

Marina looked at her fingers knitted together on her lap. "Mother isn't my real family. She just took me in because I needed a home." She met his eyes and saw the sadness in them. "But now I belong to you and you to me. I have no one else."

Dmitri dragged his thumb along her cheek. "Dear Marina. You do have someone else. You have God. He's been your Father when you had no earthly father. And He will bind our family together. No matter what happens, He will guard over us and protect our family. You must trust Him for that."

"Will He bring you home?"

Dmitri smiled and kissed her sweetly, gently. "You can count on it."

Edward Neumann crouched next to a gnarled oak tree, his eyes trained on a small clearing twenty yards in front of him, and wondered how he'd come to despise spring.

As a kid in upstate New York, the thaw and the breaking of the Schoharie River brought the promise of lazy days of fishing and cool dips when the temperature soared. He loved the thick smell of overturned earth as his father and brothers plowed the soil in the fields, and at times, he ached for the feel of cold, rich dirt filling the pores of his hands. Somewhere deep in his farmer's heart, he knew he should love spring.

Unfortunately, spring in this swatch of northern Poland, thirty kilometers from Lodz, meant mud, cold, and a rotting food supply.

A leftover breath of winter wind hissed through the Polish forest and raised the hair on his neck. He shivered despite the leather coat. His fingers felt wooden, and he hoped he still had a grip on the trigger of the US carbine rifle he poised on his shoulder. Mud and grime and cold had long since soaked through his worn wool pants and found the hole in his leather boots.

But the cold that saturated his bones emanated from within. A cold that on inky-dark, frigid nights weakened his tenuous hold on faith and nudged him further into despair.

At the moment, however, he clutched a death grip on the only thing that mattered—hope.

For you, Katrina.

Around him, an eerie quiet pervaded the forest. No birds chirping. No branches cracked. The low sun boiled crimson along the treetops and turned the birch trees blood red. Edward glanced behind him and easily made out Marek, the upper-class Pole who had, some six months prior, escaped the net around *Warszawa* and joined the Farmer's National Army. His cool demeanor while he assessed the clearing betrayed a nobleman's posture, as if he were watching a performance of *Swan Lake* at *Teatr Norodowy.*

Edward held up a hand to Marek, then pointed to Raina, who'd taken a position across the forest. He could barely make out the blond's face, but her quick wave settled relief in his heart. Her team was in place.

The song of a mockingbird brought his gaze left, to Simon, the RAF Hurricane pilot who'd barely escaped a fiery landing on the border of Estonia. Fleeing from Estonians loyal to Germany, Simon joined the Polish resistance. The two-way radio he'd secreted with him sent Edward to his knees in gratitude, even more so when he discovered the Brit was a fellow believer. Edward had to admit, even after crawling through sodden leaves and old snow, Simon still looked the Englishman—clean shaven, tidy. Bringing a touch of class to their ragtag partisan unit.

Marek signaled all clear—his scouts had scoured the south end of the forest and come up clean. Edward nodded. He raised his hand and directed Wladek and Stefan, two teenaged Poles who had the courage of the entire Third Reich, to enter the clearing. In the middle, glinting like precious rubies, lay two metal canisters. Edward prayed they indeed included clothes and food—maybe some canned meat or even sugar—along with weapons and ammo. He'd noticed Anna Lechon's bony knees protruding from her pants, and too many of his fighters' sweaters were held together with twine. Most of all, he hated to see the pale moons under young Anna's wide brown eyes. She reminded him, painfully, of his little niece back home.

And of the Polish Jews he'd seen beaten and forced into boxcars. So much like his own ancestors—accused, tortured, murdered because of their beliefs.

Anna even reminded him occasionally of Katrina. Brave in her frailty. Brave as the Nazis lined her up against a wall.

Brave unto death.

Edward blinked away the brutal images that never lurked far from the surface of his mind. He positioned the gun into his shoulder and watched with coiled breath while his two faithful partisans dashed out from cover.

The wind froze as time ticked away in their steps. More than once, a well-hidden dispatch of SS men and their dogs had ambushed a Resistance unit.

The boys reached the supply barrels and attacked them with vigor. The muscles in Edward's neck pulsed, but his breath released slowly as he watched the young men open the first barrel and raise the shiny black barrel of a British "Sten." The Poles would assemble the pieces into submachine guns. *Thanks, Colonel Stone.* When Stefan opened the second barrel, Edward blessed his director for his golden heart. Stefan held up a can of coffee, and Edward could nearly taste it hit his mouth—bitter, hot, smelling of home. Stefan turned and looked directly at him, a wide grin on his youthful face.

Edward nodded, feeling relief rush through him. Maybe this spring would bring the seeds of hope. Of victory.

The crack of a rifle shattered the crisp air. Edward choked on his relief as Stefan jerked, then crumpled to his knees. Another shot sent Wladek airborne. He landed ten feet from the canister. Reeling, Edward scanned the forest, searching for the black coats of Nazi SS men. Nothing but barren trees and shadow. His partisans however, dressed in rags of all colors, stood out like stars in the night sky.

Oh, how he hated spring.

"Let's get out of here!" Simon screamed into his ear. He fisted Edward's worn coat.

The canister pinged as another shot hit. Edward went weak at the site of Stefan crawling between the containers, his face screwed up in pain. *Oh dear Lord, please, no! The boy was still alive!*

Simon read his thoughts. "You must leave him! Now!"

Edward turned to him. "Go!" he hissed. He trained his eyes on Stefan, tasting bile at the look of terror on the youth's face. What had he gotten them into?

The spongy forest floor swallowed Simon's footsteps. Across the meadow, Edward saw Raina had also abandoned her post, like the good soldier he'd trained her to be. *Head home, fast and covertly. At all costs, don't let the enemy find you.* They all knew too much about other partisan units to be taken alive. *Run, Raina!*

Marek had also fled, taking Anna. Only Edward knew the eighteen-year-old girl had escaped from the Warsaw Ghetto, a secret he'd take with him to the grave. *"God of Israel, watch over your children."* He whitened his grip on his rifle and trained his eyes on Stefan. "I won't leave you, kid."

Not like he had Katrina. Never again. *At all costs.*

He crouched in the soggy earth, listening to his partisans flee, hearing gunshots, tasting despair. As the noise of barking dogs ricocheted through the forest and darkness hooded the sky, Edward felt the fingers of failure close in around him.

So much for spring.

ALSO FROM

BARBOUR PUBLISHING

Hidden Things
by Andrea Boeshaar
ISBN 1-58660-970-X

To face her future, Kylie must discover her mother's past. But secrets of the past bring Kylie to a God who knows all.

The Unfolding
by Jim and Terri Kraus
ISBN 1-58660-859-2

Annie Hamilton doesn't expect her life to change dramatically when she opens her modest home to a rootless and pregnant neighbor. But when the young woman abandons her newborn son, Annie summons her courage and decides to raise the baby as her own. All is well—until the day the birth mother returns to claim her child.

Take Two
by Debra White Smith
ISBN 1-59310-113-9

An east Texas widow and her son, whose wife abandoned him, find opportunities for loving a second time around. Will they take the risk?

Available wherever books are sold.